WITHDRAWN

Louis Simpson

Ships Going
into the Blue

ESSAYS AND NOTES
ON POETRY

Ann Arbor

THE UNIVERSITY OF MICHIGAN PRESS

Copyright © by the University of Michigan 1994
All rights reserved
Published in the United States of America by
The University of Michigan Press
Manufactured in the United States of America
⊗Printed on acid-free paper
1997   1996   1995   1994   4   3   2   1

A CIP catalogue record for this book is available from the British Library.

Library of Congress Cataloging-in-Publication Data

Simpson, Louis Aston Marantz, 1923–
    Ships going into the blue : essays and notes on poetry / Louis
Simpson.
        p.   cm.—(Poets on poetry)
    Includes bibliographical references and index.
    ISBN 0-472-09559-5 (alk. paper).—ISBN 0-472-06559-9 (pbk. :
alk. paper)
    1. Simpson, Louis Aston Marantz, 1923–   —Aesthetics.
2. Poetics. 3. Poetry.   I. Title.   II. Series.
PS3537.I75Z47   1994
809.1—dc20   94-16874
                                                         CIP

For Miriam,
il migliore lettore

Contents

I

A Walk with Bashō

A Wooden Bowl

When, on my travels, I tell people where I live, "Lon Guy-land" they say and smile, as though talking through the nose explains why a poet couldn't possibly live there. Friendly's and Finast . . . houses stamped out with a cookie cutter . . . the "manor" house on its "builder's acre" like an elephant on a pea patch. People whose only passion seems to be driving a motorboat and playing golf . . . Is there anything at all romantic about Long Island?

Romance isn't the only kind of poetry. Emerson quotes Milton's saying that "the lyric poet may drink wine and live generously, but the epic poet, he who shall sing of the gods, and their descent unto men, must drink water out of a wooden bowl." I drink water, and these streets, houses, and shopping centers are my bowl. It would be the same if I lived in Italy, or on the edge of the Australian outback, or in Sweden. People are much the same everywhere, at least in the Western world, and it is people and what they do and say that I write about, not disembodied feelings.

A striped pole leaned out from the sidewalk, moving irresistibly towards me. This was in Rome . . . I was driving a new Volkswagen when traffic came rushing in from the right, pushing me across. The pole like a barber's sign loomed up in front, angling into the street. It crumpled my left fender. A policeman walked over to look at the damage. I could see him thinking, "How did you manage to do it, stupid?"

Newsday Magazine, February 17, 1991 (there titled "A Poet's Bowl"). The poem "Waiting in the Service Station" is reprinted from *In the Room We Share* by permission of the publisher, Paragon House.

Some day this incident may take its place in a poem or essay, when I have an idea that needs it. The idea may have nothing to do with Rome. In the meantime I must wait . . . shave, dress, and face the day. One is not a poet then, and this is what people do not understand: they think that poets are different, that they are always "on," like a certain kind of actor.

I look around me, listen, and wait for the poem that needs a striped pole. Or a dented fender. Can there be anything "poetic" about waiting for your car to be fixed?

> Waiting in the service station,
> reading *Sports Illustrated,*
>
> listening to every sound
> and wondering, is it mine? . . .
>
> When they say the car is ready
> and I go to pay the bill
>
> I'm relieved, I'd pay anything
> to be out of there, on the road,
>
> moving with the traffic,
> looking at the buildings and signs:
>
> Clams'n Stuff, Scelfo Realty,
> Candi's X-Rated Dancers.

My First Acquaintance with a Poet

Does anyone remember Neville Dane? Here and there, perhaps in an old Oscar Williams anthology, you may come across a poem by Dane. But he is not mentioned in any recent history of American poetry. This strikes me as an injustice, for Neville Dane was an innovator—he was forty years ahead of his time.

I knew Neville Dane: he worked in the bookstore at Columbia in the early 1940s when I was an undergraduate. I hasten to say that I didn't know him well; nobody did. I had a friend who came across a short story by a Neville Dane in an anthology dated 1928. He asked Neville if he was the same person, and he said he wasn't. If he had been he would have been considerably older than he appeared to be. Now and then he would let fall a remark that suggested that he had been around a long time and had rubbed elbows with famous people. From what he said, he knew E. E. Cummings personally. But he didn't elaborate—he was enigmatic.

I talked to him about poetry, and he said the trouble with mine was that I was trying to "say" something. Poetry shouldn't be "about" anything. Then he published a book of poems. Some of us had thought Neville rather funny: we were sure he was the writer in the old anthology, pretending to be young. We imitated his enigmatic smile. But now he had published a book, and it had been reviewed on the front page of the *New York Times Book Review*. A curtain descended between

New York Times Book Review, March 1, 1992 (there titled "The Stupefying Rhythms of Neville Dane").

him and us. If what the reviewer said was true, Neville Dane belonged to the ages.

It was unheard of for a book of poetry, and one by an unknown author, to receive this kind of attention. But *Angel Telegrams* had been published handsomely, with a blurb by Cummings: he praised the "ecstatic, Blakean quality" of Dane's verse. There were other fulsome notices by well-known names, and what the blurb writers said was repeated in reviews that appeared in newspapers and magazines all over the country.

The next time I saw Neville he was married. I ran into him on Broadway and he invited me to come up and meet his wife; they had just had a baby. The apartment had six rooms, high ceilings, and a view of the Hudson. They were paying a very high rent, $175 a month, but apparently they could afford it. Neville's wife was young and pretty, and the baby looked very big. Neville wasn't a big man himself; he was on the small side. I thought how lucky he was, with his fame, a wife who obviously adored him and a son. The future could not have looked brighter.

I went to the library recently and found a copy of *Angel Telegrams*. The last time it had been taken out, said the slip at the back, was in September 1956, the year after Allen Ginsberg read "Howl" at the Six Gallery in San Francisco. The date on the slip struck me as significant; an old order was changing, giving place to a new.

The poems in *Angel Telegrams* look simple:

> God first I saw,
> Then Mother, Father.
> Angel I was,
> akin to neither.
>
> Voices I heard,
> And one became.
> All else dreary,
> Babel, self-same.

The writing is far from simple. In every stanza, the end word of the third line rhymes in reverse with the end word of the first line. The French call this *rime retournée*—it is listed in Larousse's *Encyclopédie Littéraire,* with a credit to Neville Dane as the inventor of the form. I believe this to be the only instance on record of the French having credited an American with having invented anything.

Dane's reverse rhymes aren't always exact—sometimes he bends his rule a little. To be the exact reverse of "dreary," "I heard," should have an "r" between "h" and "I." But verse isn't an exact science, however hard we try to make it so, and this is quibbling. All the reverse rhymes in *Angel Telegrams,* and there were hundreds, must have been very hard to find: they must have cost Dane many a weary night with a dictionary. If, as they say, genius is an infinite capacity for taking pains, Neville Dane was a genius.

There was hardly any meaning or content in the poems— Dane was after pure poetry. As I've said, he was way ahead of his time. In those days people didn't know that there are really no such things as meaning and content, that these are just fictions, that there is no reality outside language, nothing to which it refers. But in that primitive, prestructuralist age Neville Dane had discovered that everything is language, and language has no meaning.

To understand what happened next, one must know how it was to be a poet in the 1940s. Poets then were isolated. There were no creative writing programs and poetry-writing workshops; they just started writing on their own. Poets today begin by enrolling in a creative-writing program in any one of a hundred universities. There they will receive criticism from a group and learn how to avoid making mistakes. After receiving a Master of Fine Arts degree they will teach writing workshops and keep in touch with others who do the same. They will support one another and pass on news of available grants and fellowships. If one of them should be so lucky as to become a member of an Academy or Institute, he or she will do everything that he or she can do to bring in his or her friends.

Neville Dane's was a "silent generation." In the 1940s poets went it alone, and he went way out—on a limb.

If you want to remove any idea, content, element of narrative from the poem—to make it, as Mallarmé said, as unlike prose as possible—where are you going to stop? Why not just have the poem make sounds? Another poet might have hesitated, but whatever one may think of Dane, he was sincere in his beliefs. With his second book he carried out an experiment that went beyond anything anyone, even E. E. Cummings, had tried. I haven't even found anything like it by the Dadaists. Dane wanted the reader to pay attention to the sound values of poetry, to read language as language, not as a vehicle for ideas. He wanted every vocable to count, to slow up the reader and force him or her to hear the sounds. So he put an exlamation mark after every letter. I think his choice of the exclamation mark must have been guided by what Cummings said about the "ecstatic" quality of his writing.

The whole of *W!a!l!k!s! i!n! E!d!e!n!* was like that. It must have been very difficult to write all those exclamation marks; it must have worn out the key on his typewriter. And, sure enough, Dane's publisher had a lot of trouble with the printer; rumor had it that the man demanded double rates. But Dane had a big reputation on the strength of his first book, so *W!a!l!k!s! i!n! E!d!e!n!* was published with some fanfare—and fell flat.

The critics were harsh. I recall what one of them said in the *Times.* I kept the review: "Neville Dane's second book marks an advance in the art of verse: it puts him in the avant-garde, and so far ahead that he cannot be followed, for any poet who tries to follow will immediately be seen for what he is, a mere copycat. Mr. Dane has put an exclamation mark after every letter of his poems. Yes, e!v!e!r!y! l!e!t!t!e!r! Let the reader try to visualize the effect in a book of 1!2!8! p!a!g!e!s! It is stupefying, like looking for a long time at mascara running down a face. After three poems I found that I had to lie down.

"But though no one may follow, Mr. Dane's course for the future is clear. And there's no stepping back ... to do so would be to admit that his method is wrong. He must continue to write lines like:

I!n! t!h!e! g!a!r!d!e!n! o!f! E!d!e!n!
T!h!e!r!e! a!r!e! f!i!g!s! o!n! e!a!c!h! b!o!u!g!h!

"We may expect poems with a comma after every letter . . .
a book of letters and semicolons. And how about asterisks and
the figure on the keyboard that indicates a number, a #? I can
see him entering a phase of doubt, every letter followed by ?

T?o? b?e? o?r? n?o?t? t?o? b?e? . . .

"If I were Mr. Dane, however, I'd bypass the $. Readers
might construe this to mean that he has sold out$. I'll
say this for him: this could not possibly happen: he will not
gain monetary or any other kind of reward. Most readers
dislike poetry—even poets, as a poet has said, dislike it. How
much more will they dislike poetry they cannot read. Neville
Dane is fated to be unique. If Isaac D'Israeli were alive he
would have pounced: what a fine specimen this poet would
have made in his collection of literary curiosities."

As rapidly as Dane had risen, that swift was his fall. The
reviewer was right: there was no way for him to abandon his
method without acknowledging that he'd been wrong, in fact,
very foolish. Poets may be many things, and we've seen them:
drunk, dishonest, lecherous, irate, illiterate. But they can't
afford to look foolish. As far as I know Dane never published
another book. Once I did come across a poem by him in a little
magazine. He had read the review I've quoted and had taken
up the challenge:

*I$ too$ have seen the$ best minds$ of
my generation*

It continued in this vein, but I found it unreadable.
I saw him once more. I was in the Village with a friend.
We went to a restaurant and were in the middle of ordering
when a party of a dozen men and women entered. With
them was Neville Dane. He was very much in charge. He sat
at the head of the table and talked in a loud voice, so as to be

heard by the people seated at the far end. He was recommending the paella. He told anecdotes about life in Greenwich Village.

I didn't go over and speak to him. He was busy. Besides, I didn't think we would have much to say to each other.

Humane Letters

I'll say this for Amsterdam, they allowed their young instructors to teach courses in literature. At other places it was nothing but freshman composition. In my second year at Amsterdam I was given a section of Great Books and Ideas. The course met four times a week and covered a great deal of ground, beginning with Homer and ending with Kafka.

Some of the books we taught were way beyond us. I stayed awake one night on the train back from Boston with a splitting headache—I'd been visiting a friend in Cambridge—trying to understand Spinoza before the class that met at nine in the morning. I couldn't follow the propositions and proofs, but I thought I might be able to do something with ideas such as, "When the mind imagines its wants of power it is saddened by that fact." The next morning as I discussed with my freshmen what Spinoza had to say about "The Origins and Nature of the Emotions" I became rather emotional myself. They sat holding the brown paper bags in which they'd brought their lunch from Brooklyn or the Bronx, and let me have my say. My performance must have struck them as manic. They had no feelings about Spinoza one way or the other. Obviously he was important or he wouldn't have been on the list. Great Books and Ideas was a requirement, like the number of laps you had to swim in the pool, on the way to the good life. They tackled the assignments, passed the course, and went on to a career in medicine, law, engineering, or business management.

Gordon Knowles also had a section of Great Books and Ideas. He and I used to lunch at the Green Dragon—we lived

Gettysburg Review, Spring 1990.

in furnished rooms and didn't have brown paper bags with a sandwich wrapped by loving hands. His people were somewhere in Wisconsin, and the only family I had were some aunts, an uncle who was a pharmacist and worked behind a counter at Whelan's, a block from Times Square, and a female cousin who had married a man in a "supply house." He was very quiet and his name was Henry. I hardly knew these men, and my female relatives weren't able to throw any light on the things that bothered a young man.

Over chicken chow mein or shrimp chop suey, or the combination (with fried rice and egg roll), Gordon and I discussed the great books. Every week we encountered ideas that were new to us. There was no method to teaching in those days, no "theory"—you just pitched into the text and tried to understand it, and explained it as best you could. I am not making any claims for our understanding, nor do I mean to attack the currently fashionable theoretical approaches to literature and lament the disappearance of the author and the decline of Western civilization. Civilization is always in decline, that's what makes it so interesting. Give me a losing cause every time. Now that communism is failing I think I may be able to get through *Das Kapital.*

Gordon wasn't the kind of man you expected to find at Amsterdam. I think this was why they hired him; they were under pressure by the trustees to attract students from more distant parts of the continent than Brooklyn and Staten Island. An instuctor with Gordon's qualifications—solid grades and a Ph.D. from Michigan State, and a splendid record as an athlete—would help to give the college a more American image.

He couldn't believe his luck. He said, "There are men I knew back at Michigan who'd give their eye teeth to be at Amsterdam, teaching Great Books and Ideas."

There were people I knew too, where I came from, who would probably have envied me. Alone at night, sitting over a great book, the moon shining through my window, I would feel exceptionally blessed. But I didn't let people know how I felt. Gordon let everyone know, and this didn't go down well with other instructors. They didn't feel so grateful to be at Amsterdam—they thought they deserved to be there, or else at Harvard. And they didn't feel at all grateful when they thought how little they were being paid for their labors. When Gordon expressed the kind of enthusiasm in the office he shared with three other instructors that he expressed to me over lunch, they exchanged unbelieving glances.

You might think that youthful innocence and enthusiasm would have appealed to the senior members. Not so. They prided themselves on being worldly. They wrote for the *Nation* and *Partisan Review;* they had connections with publishing houses; one who taught the Renaissance was an old friend of Marlene Dietrich. These men who had passed their lives among books and ideas craved diversion. And Gordon wasn't diverting—he was in dead earnest. His favorite novel was *Look Homeward, Angel.*

There was a model boy in the department: Francisco de Viana. The de Vianas were an old Brazilian family and said to be rich. Francisco was goodlooking . . . he bore a marked resemblance to Tyrone Power. And he was knowledgeable—he appeared to be an authority on every subject from the Albigensian heresy to epileptic patterns in Dostoyevsky's novels. He preferred to be silent, but when he spoke everyone listened.

Francisco sometimes stood in for Professor Corby, taking his classes when Corby was unavoidably detained. Hallowell Corby was the most distinguished member of the department, a critic with an international reputation. Francisco was seen having lunch with Corby at the Faculty Club, and it became known that he had been to the Corbys' for dinner when W. H. Auden was there. We regarded Francisco rather as his companions must have regarded Aeneas when he came back from talking to a god.

I felt sorry for Gordon. When quips and quotes were flying around the office he sat smiling woodenly. This was noticed and the quips flew faster. He stared down at the student papers he was correcting, too busy writing "agr" and "sp" in the margins to take part in an intellectual feast. From time to time he smiled broadly to show that he wasn't being excluded . . . just too busy, that's all. After a while he picked up the papers, put them in his briefcase, and left.

He was walking in front of me in the direction of the subway. Some undergraduates were throwing a football. It rolled to his feet and he returned it with a long throw. I caught up to him. "Hello, Joe," he said. "I miss football. We had a great team at Michigan. At the end of the day a few of us in the department would go out and throw a ball. It relaxed the mind."

He held no resentment against the bright ones who engaged in conversations that were above his head and who, he was aware—he wasn't stupid, I don't want to give that impression—laughed at him behind his back. One day Marty Halpern called him a fool to his face. Gordon blushed. Then he walked out of the room.

I had lunch with him the next day. I was angry at the way he let them treat him. I said, "You shouldn't let them get away with it."

He said, "We share the same office, and I never have much to say. I suppose it gets on their nerves. Let's face it, they're a lot cleverer than I am."

Corby spoke to me one day in the hall. "Joseph, Mrs. Corby and I would like you to come to dinner. It will be just a small gathering, nothing formal."

On the day and at the hour appointed I arrived at the Corbys' apartment on Charles Street.

People see themselves as better or worse than they are. The fashion these days, at least in writing, is to make yourself out to be void of feelings and principles, just the shell of a human being, going through the motions. This seems to sell copies at the bookstore. But though it may not sell copies I must confess that I was a pretty decent fellow. I had no intention of sucking up to the Corbys. There were more important things than "making it." To be invited to their home, singled out among the instructors, was a great honor. On the other hand, I didn't intend to say a thing I didn't believe. I could always get a job in a stockroom. I'd once worked for an import-export firm, wrapping stockings with small imperfections, "seconds," in cellophane so that they looked like new. I was proud of my skill with cartons and sticking paper.

Beside Hallowell and Gertrude Corby, present that evening were the Harveys—he was in Romance languages; a man named Bromfield who edited a series of classics in paperback, and Francisco de Viana, escorting a young woman with long legs and auburn hair. She was a model, and the Corbys were obviously pleased to be entertaining such a glamorous type. They plied her with questions about the fashion business.

Everything went smoothly at dinner. Mrs. Corby asked me how I liked being at Amsterdam and I said I was enjoying it very much. The model, Francisco's date, was sitting across from me; she had a lot more on her mind than the fashion business. She was taking courses in anthropology at Columbia; she thought the Samoan islanders weren't as Margaret Mead described them, free of the inhibitions about sex that plagued young Americans. The note-taker had been taken for a ride by Samoan girls with lively imaginations and a semse of humor.

Corby had heard our conversation. "That can't be so," he said. "Mead is to be on the list of Great Books and Ideas. I'm sorry to differ with you, but I think you've been misinformed."

The auburn-haired anthropologist winked at me. It almost made up for the rest of the evening.

We were having coffee and liqueurs in the living room. Professor Harvey asked how things were with the Department of English, and Corby said we were expanding. "Our new people," he said, "are very good. That is, two of them are. One," with a nod in my direction, "is Mr. Turner. The other was unable to be with us this evening. His wife is having a baby. Of the third, the less said the better."

The third was Gordon Knowles. Corby proceeded to explain why the less said the better. Knowles was a ridiculous man, not at all the Amsterdam type. He wore white buckskins, and he had been heard to say that Eisenhower was a great man.

There wasn't much I could say in Gordon's defense; it was true that he wasn't bright—he said so himself.

Where had the oaf come from? "Some place," Corby said

with a dismissive gesture, "out west." I had come from some place myself. As I heard them taking such pleasure in Gordon Knowles's naïveté I felt that, under it all, I too was not the Amsterdam College type.

I have been told that my face reveals my feelings, and it must have done so that evening, for a few days later when Corby and I met in the hall he did not say how pleased he and Mrs. Corby were to have me to dinner, he merely nodded. He was usually distant, in keeping with his role of *grand seigneur,* royalty traveling incognito under the guise of a professor, but still . . .

I was on my way to the library. Corby and Francisco were standing on the path, in profile against the facade with its names cut in stone, with extra space between the names like passengers traveling in first class: Aeschylus . Thucydides . Hippocrates . Plato . Justinian . Aquinas . Chaucer . Newton.

Corby saw me approaching. He raised his right hand and beckoned.

"What do you think," he said. "Is this man Salinger as good as everyone says?"

It was one of his test questions. According as you gave the right answer or the wrong one, your stock would rise or fall. But he didn't wait for my answer. His attention was diverted to the cigar Francisco was taking from a case. The case was of silver, the cigar elegantly thin.

"May I look at that?" Corby said, and Francisco handed over the case. It had a design on the cover. "Isn't this splendid," Corby said. He held out the case so I could see the design: an Indian standing with his legs crossed and leaning on a spear, facing an alligator that had its jaws wide open. It was rather careless of the Indian.

Corby turned to Francisco, who was lighting the cigar with a lighter as expensive as the case. "Are they as good as Maria's?"

A woman named Maria who smoked cigars? Then I understood: not "belonging to Maria," but the brand of cigar Hans Castorp used to smoke. I had read *The Magic Mountain.*

Francisco smiled. Corby was referring to something he and Francisco had talked about, some private joke, and I was expected not to understand. Corby's next remark confirmed my suspicion. Turning to me he said, "It's what a Maria looked like, wouldn't you say?"

"No," I said. " 'Maria Mancinis' were black. This is more like a 'Light of Asia.' "

It was the kind of answer you only think of afterwards, on the staircase as the French say. But on this occasion my timing was right. I went my way, leaving them to stare.

It was a costly victory: I had spoiled Corby's little game, turned the tables on him, and in front of Francisco. Though Francisco would never let on, I am sure he enjoyed seeing the great man put down. He had no more liking for Corby than I did—he was only pretending to like him till he could step into his shoes.

From that day there were no more remarks of favor from Corby . . . no more "Josephs." When he had to speak to me it was "Mr. Turner." In the fall Gordon and I were not given sections of Great Books and Ideas, only classes of freshman composition, and at the end of the semester our contracts were not renewed.

> "And everybody praised the Duke
>   Who this great fight did win."
> "But what good came of it at last?"
>   Quoth little Peterkin.
> "Why, that I cannot tell," said he.
> "But 'twas a famous victory."

Hallowell Corby died full of years. The following December, at the annual meeting of the Modern Language Association, Francisco de Viana attacked "the cult of personality" in language studies, using Corby as a point of departure.

He read passages from Corby's *Humane Letters* and said that they merely expressed the emotions of the writer. The time for this kind of impressionism had passed. Today the world looked to science; if we who dealt in the humanities were to be competitive, we must approach our work in a scientific spirit. What did we actually know? Language. One word led to another, one metaphor to another. As Saussure had said, there was nothing beyond language, no "meaning" to which it referred—we made all the meanings ourselves. Hallowell Corby's "great ideas" had no reality. Outside its expression in words, our thought was simply a vague, shapeless mass.

The ghost of Hallowell Corby hung before the audience, a vague, shapeless mass. They had begun to murmur. One voice carried: "If there is no meaning, then what you say has no meaning."

The lecturer thanked the person who had just spoken: his comment had brought them to the inescapable conclusion. The study of language must be the study of the use of language . . . rhetoric, in short. Far from narrowing the field, as some in the audience might fear, this would bring the study of language and literature right into the heat of action.

He would let someone else make the conclusion plain. He held up a book and read:

> "I don't know what you mean by 'glory,' " Alice said.
>
> Humpty Dumpty smiled contemptuously. "Of course you don't—till I tell you. I meant 'There's a nice knock-down argument for you!' "
>
> "But 'glory' doesn't mean 'a nice knock-down argument,' " Alice objected.
>
> "When *I* use a word," Humpty Dumpty said in rather a scornful tone, "it means just what I choose it to mean—neither more nor less."
>
> "The question is," said Alice, "whether you *can* make words mean different things."
>
> "The question is," said Humpty Dumpty, "which is to be master—that's all."

I liked northern California: the redwoods, the haunting mixture of sunshine and fog. The teaching was easier than it had been in New York: you didn't have the kind of student who put up his hand and said, "Shouldn't we first be discussing Hegel?" What right did a freshman who brought his lunch in a paper bag have to be talking about Hegel? There were bright young people in California, but they weren't well-informed—it wasn't hard to keep a step ahead of them. And the girls were a lot better looking.

This became a problem until I married. My wife and I bought a house with a separate cabin in which I could write. It was on a down slope, looking up at the road and the cars and legs going by: a pair of swollen ankles and a walking stick— the old man who lived by himself; two skinny legs on a skateboard—the kid from two houses up; a pair of shapely legs in a miniskirt—Marcia, the Kingsley's older daughter. I was lucky to be here: in New York I'd have been looking at the air shaft or rows of windows.

But everyone, as the Romans used to say, wants to live "in the world of the upper floors." That is where you meet interesting people. At a party in Manhattan you were likely to meet Norman Mailer or Gore Vidal. But not J. D. Salinger. I imagined that he lived much as I did, out of the world. It gave me hope for my own writing.

Recently I looked again at the pages in *The Magic Mountain* that changed my life. A few words can make all the difference. Soldiers and sailors know this, so do people on trial for their lives, and so, I would say, do most women. But we who trade in words find it hard to believe that words are real and can change people's lives. Perhaps because we trade in them.

There it was: "Maria Mancini . . . Costs little or nothing, nineteen pfennigs in plain colors." On the previous page . . . "He had a cigar in his mouth, a very black one."

At the end of the book Hans Castorp has switched to a different brand called "Light of Asia . . . mouse-gray in color with a blue band."

I had been right all down the line.

"The Precinct Station"—Structure and Idea

In the early 1950s I worked as an associate editor for a publishing house in Manhattan. The work consisted mainly of reading novels, my feet propped on the bottom desk drawer. There was another associate, the man I have called Mike in "The Precinct Station." Mike wrote articles on jazz; he was writing a novel, and he was an alcoholic. The head editor had a great deal of respect for Mike as a future novelist, and so put up with his coming late to work and not finishing assignments. The head editor would sometimes ask me to do Mike's work for him.

Mike was sleeping with Lorna. She was married, but this seemed to be no obstacle. Then, one night, Lorna was in the emergency ward at Bellevue and Mike was at a police station, under arrest for attempted homocide. In the version that went the rounds, Lorna had picked up a carving knife and Mike had tried to take it away from her, inflicting a wound that required twenty stitches. There was some uncertainty about what she had meant to do with the carving knife. The head editor had gone to the station and bailed Mike out. In the sequel Lorna refused to press charges, and Mike continued to work for the publishing house until his absences became flagrant and the head editor regretfully let him go.

Thirty years after the event I wrote a narrative poem about

Ecstatic Occasions, Expedient Forms: 65 Leading Contemporary Poets Select and Comment on Their Poems, ed. David Lehman (New York: Macmillan, 1987).

it. My writing usually takes its origin from an actual incident, character, or uttered speech. I included myself, the narrator, as a character in the story. I described my job in publishing, and my first meeting with Lorna. It was in the White Horse Tavern. She was with her husband and Mike introduced us. A few minutes later, in order to illustrate some point in a story she was telling, she unbuttoned her blouse and showed us her breasts. The nipples were small and pink, like tea roses.

I wrote other incidents, as though I were writing a novel. They were strung together like beads on a string. I told myself that I was making leaps, as in cinematography, but what was harder to explain away was the flatness of the language. Then, after many drafts, it occurred to me that the narrator was jealous of Mike, jealous of the sexual favors granted by Lorna to this alcoholic who was habitually late for work. Jealous, too, of the friendship of Mike and the head editor, who would ask the narrator to do Mike's work for him. The narrator had been imposed upon—this poem was his revenge.

From the beginning, the first draft, there had been eight lines that stood out from the rest, describing the precinct station. Here the language was not flat—there were striking images and a compelling rhythm. I had placed these lines in the middle of the poem, but when I saw that it was the narrator's frame of mind that interested me, I moved the lines to the end. They were the objective correlative of his feelings, envy and resentment, lurking like the cockroach under the baseboard at the precinct station.

But would the reader see this? There has been a failure of imagination among readers of poetry. They think that poetry has to be "sincere," by which they mean talking about oneself, one's family, one's friends. They don't want anything to have been "made up," and as for poetry setting out to give plea-sure, these latter-day Puritans dislike it wholeheartedly. They want sermons in church, the Church of True Confession, or the Church of Supreme Meditation, whatever. But I am inter-ested in the variety and sensation of real ideas. Poetry makes ideas seem real by removing the detritus of fact and substitut-ing something else that is more to the point.

I did not trust the reader to see the underlying motif. But it would be truer to say that I did not feel that I had carried it off. The incidents, even with this explanation, were strung together; the language remained flat. Something, however, might be salvaged: the part about the precinct station. I amputated this and sent it to the *Georgia Review*. They published it in the fall of 1984.

26th Precinct Station

One night Jake telephoned
to say, "Mike has stabbed Lorna."
He wanted me to call his lawyer . . .
couldn't do it himself, he was tied up.

I called the lawyer, who had just come in
from seeing *Kismet*. We shared a taxi.
All the way down to the station
he kept humming "And This Is My Beloved."

Lorna recovered, and wrote a novel.
Mike married and went to live in Rome.
Jake Harmon died. But I remember
the 26th Precinct Station.

A black woman in a yellow wig,
a purple skirt, and stiletto heels;
a pickpocket; a cripple
arrested for indecent exposure.

The naked light bulb; the crack in the wall
that loops like the Mississippi at Vicksburg;
the shadow of the cockroach
under the baseboard, lurking, gathering his nerve.

When you have published a poem I think you should leave it alone. Rewriting lines and changing titles, revising so as to have a different meaning—the kind of thing Auden did—shows an excessive care to refurbish the past and present oneself in the best possible light. The revised poem is true neither to what one used to write and think nor what one thinks and writes in the present—a flavorless hybrid.

There is always the exception, however, and perhaps in this instance the rule does not apply, for revision of "26th Precinct Station" took place within a few months of the poem's being published, so that publication was merely an interruption of the writing.

I still wasn't satisfied. The lines describing the precinct station still seemed strong, and the lines that came before were as good as I could make them, with a happy, ironic touch—the song title, "And This Is My Beloved." But there was too much explanation and, at the same time, not enough. Something appeared to be missing. I felt that I had cheated the reader and myself—myself being the more seriously injured party.

It has been said before, and has to be said again: structure, or plot, depends on feeling—not the other way round.

I examined my feelings again, going back to the facts of the case. A light flashed on, revealing a fact so obvious that I had not seen it. In the poem I had myself visiting the precinct station. But I had not visited the station—it was the head editor who did so and who got Mike out of trouble. Could this be the key I was looking for? I discarded the lines that described my going to the station and wrote four lines saying that I didn't go and someone else went and bailed Mike out.

The lines about the station now had a reason for being, and for being as they were, grotesque. The naked light; the crack in the wall; the cockroach; the woman in the yellow wig, a threatening female; the pickpocket, one who lived by stealing; the cripple arrested for indecent exposure—were projections of the narrator's unacted desire and his fearful imagining of what would happen if he did act. He had not taken his chances with sex and possibly violence, and therefore, like Coleridge's albatross, the precinct station was hung about his neck and he was compelled to see it again and again.

I wrote a new beginning in four lines that came easily, seeming to write themselves. I changed Lorna to Nancy for the sound of the line, and "stiletto heels" to "heels like stilettos" for the rhythm. Though the purist might object that "stiletto heels" was a standard phrase, I felt that rhythm must take precedence.

When Mike stuck a knife in Nancy
I didn't go to the precinct station
to bail him out—someone else did.
But ever since I've had an idea

of what it's like: a woman in a yellow wig,
a purple skirt, and heels like stilettos;
a pickpocket; a cripple
arrested for indecent exposure;

the naked light; the crack in the wall
that loops like the Mississippi at Vicksburg;
the shadow of the cockroach
under the baseboard, lurking, gathering his nerve.

This is a long explanation for twelve lines of verse. But the important struggles need not take place on a wide canvas—they may happen in a corner. The process I went through in arriving at the final structure of this poem would apply to the writing of all poems. I had to be open to all possibilities, willing to start again from scratch, to say to myself, No. I did not do or feel the things the poem says I did and felt. I'll have to try something else.

There have been writers who did not believe in rewriting. They argue that the first step has been placed in the universe—it is there forever, unchangeable. But the second draft of the poem, and the third—are they not also placed in the universe? So the question of which draft is the best—that is, which moves people most strongly, seems most true—is still to be decided. The best draft may not be the first but the tenth, or the fortieth. The wish simply to speak and have it accepted as poetry is one with the child's wish to utter a cry and be obeyed.

The structure of the poem depends on an idea, and the more the idea proceeds from the character of the poet, the more it compels the poem into a certain form. It may take some examination of one's feelings, and much rewriting, to discover what they mean.

An Explosive Moment

I still have my "credentials," a blue card from the John F. Kennedy Space Center with a picture of an American eagle landing on the moon. On the reverse it says, "The National Aeronautics and Space Administration welcomes you to the launch of Apollo 11, the first mission planned to land Man on the Moon and return him safely to Earth."

NASA had invited a few writers to Cape Kennedy to observe the moon launch. Norman Mailer wrote a whole book about it . . . I wrote sixteen lines of a poem. For twenty years I've felt that I owe NASA a refund for my airline ticket and hotel accommodations.

In the section of bleachers where I was seated there were governors of the states and their wives. Directly in front of me, on the tier below, sat the wife of the governor of a Southern state. Louisiana? Alabama? She was beautifully got up for the occasion in a gown and wide hat.

Some minutes before the launching I went to the refreshment booth to get a soda. There was a crowd around the booth. I gave my order in a loud voice and the woman in the booth looked at me. I handed a dollar to a man in front and he passed it on. She seemed to hesitate for a moment, then she reached down and picked out a can. Later I would think of the right words for her look: she saw me coming.

The can had a dent in it. But what did it matter and I was in a hurry to get back to my seat. People were taking snapshots . . . the moment was approaching. A flame appeared beneath the rocket on its platform a mile away. At this mo-

Newsday Magazine, July 9, 1989.

ment I pulled the tab on my can and the contents exploded, spraying across the back of the governor's wife . . . a splatter of brown across the white material.

I remember the rocket climbing . . . so slowly at first that it seems suspended in midair. Then it gathers speed and seems to curve. It disappears in the cloud cover, leaving a hole. Superimposed on this is a face in a wide hat turned toward me. Words are issuing from the face and I am trying to apologize.

This may be why the lines I wrote failed to rise to the occasion. I described the take-off:

> I saw the first men leave for the moon:
> how the rocket clawed at the ground
> at first, reluctant to lift;
> how it rose, and climbed, and curved,
> punching a round, black hole in a cloud.

But I said nothing about the historical importance of the event, nothing to compare with Neil Armstrong's words from the moon: "That's one small step for man, one giant leap for mankind." (His words, I noticed, were changed later on to make sense. The media reported him as saying "a small step for a man, a giant step for mankind.")

All I had to say was, "They will send me off to Heaven / when all I want is to live in the world." I seem to have been eager to go home. My conversation with the governor's wife may have had something to do with it.

A Leave of Absence

I had been given a grant and was able to take a year off from teaching. It was time for a change of scene. London seemed a good idea . . . there'd be no trouble finding schools for the children, always a consideration when you went abroad. We rented a flat through an ad in the *Times*. It was in Primrose Hill, close to Regent's Park and only a few minutes by bus or underground to the center of town.

We couldn't have the flat till the end of June, so we spent a week sightseeing in London, then traveled by train to Scotland. I had a friend there, Robin Lorimer, who had published my book on James Hogg, the Ettrick Shepherd.

I visited Edinburgh in order to do the research. It was March, the streets were wet and cold, and I shivered in an unheated bedsitter. On Sunday everything was closed—I spent one Scottish Sabbath in bed waiting for Monday to come. But this trip was different: thanks to the Ettrick Shepherd doors opened as if by magic and my wife and I discovered a cheerful, convivial world behind the gray stones of Auld Reekie. "Have another slice of beef," said our hostess. "No thanks," I said, "it's very good but . . ." "I didna doot the roast," she said, giving me a lesson in Scottish manners: you don't compliment the hostess on her dinner—it is always good.

We traveled to Inverness and the field of Culloden. I had read that my father's people were a branch of a clan, the Frasers, that fought in the battle. It had been a disaster, half-naked Highlanders running onto English muskets and bayonets.

Partisan Review, no. 4 (1990).

They were buried at Culloden in a mass grave. Afterwards the English hunted the rebels among the hills, and some were shipped to the colonies in chains. This may have been how my Scottish ancestor came to Jamaica.

It would have been romantic, but more likely he was a clerk who hoped to better his fortunes by keeping the books on a plantation, or a poor schoolmaster. In any case he must have been desperate: Europeans who went to the West Indies were likely to die of fever. English regiments left a trail of graves behind them when they reembarked for England. It was more dangerous fighting a tropical climate than the American colonists or the French.

We traveled across the Highlands to the Isle of Skye. Among the thistles and patches of heather you may be the first since the beginning of time to have stood in this particular spot. An immense solitude broods over the hills. There are no curtains between you and it.

We moved into the flat in Primrose Hill, found a butcher and a baker, and arranged to have milk delivered. It was a short walk to Regent's Park . . . at night the wind brought the howling of wolves in the zoo.

Primrose actually was a hill. People took their lunch there, children flew kites, and one day there was a gathering of druids in white robes. They walked in a circle waving wands and uttering incantations. Afterwards they repaired to a pub on the corner that had pictures of the mistresses of King Edward VII, grand courtesans of the turn of the century and wives whose connection with the monarch placed them above criticism. They looked down on the world with a royal air.

The pub was a meeting place for writers and people who worked for the BBC or did something in the theater. Anecdotes overheard at the bar furnished ideas for articles, television scripts, and novels.

The poet Heine said, "Don't send a poet to London." He may have been thinking of wet streets and umbrellas. But though London may not be a good place for a poet it offers many opportunities to the race that lives by its wits. A writer can make a living by writing a radio script one week, an article in the *New Statesman* the next. In the States such people are likely to find a niche in a university. With the assurance of a paycheck every fortnight they may no longer feel a compulsion to write, or they may run out of material: departmental intrigues and the lives of professors are scarcely the stuff of great fiction. The writer in the university teaches a class in *Hamlet* and goes to his study to work on his novel about a professor's affair with one of his students.

It was good to be away from the English department and rubbing elbows with men and women who moved in the world. Even scholars in England were more in tune with events than their American counterparts: there was not the separation between the life of the mind and public events that one found in the States.

There was an aspect of the English literary scene, however, that I found hard to take. A newspaper article or letter to the editor would have a hostile or sneering remark about America that was purely gratuitous or had only the most tenuous connection to the matter in hand. The "Hollywood influence" had driven out that fine, democratic institution, the English music hall, and so on. Resentment of the United States was common among Englishmen who had gone to one of the better public schools. They had been able to lord it over the lower classes and swank about in the colonies, but the Empire no longer existed and Americans now had the material advantages they used to command. They would rather see Russian tanks in the streets of Prague and Warsaw than American tourists occupying the best seats in the house.

Two thousand years after the Crucifixion Jesus was born again in Bethlehem. He grew up as he had before, an outstanding Yeshiva student and a credit to his parents. When he came to man's estate he took up public speaking and performing miracles: he healed the halt, the lame, and the blind. His fame spread throughout Israel . . . it was said that he had fed a multitude on a few biscuits and sardines. He traveled around the world, drawing crowds wherever he went.

He came to England and people flocked to the Institute of Contemporary Arts to see and hear him. They were greatly impressed, especially when he told them that he had raised the dead. When he finished speaking there was a question period. A hand went up in the audience. "We know," the Englishman said, "that you are wise beyond belief and that you have performed miracles. We are even willing to admit that you are the son of God. But where did you go to school?"

I subscribed to the London Library in St. James's Square. It was a fine library—they allowed you to take home first editions. I wasn't writing much . . . in all the time we stayed in England I wrote only one poem and it was set in the States. Heine was right, I could never be a poet in London, but I could get a lot of reading done. And I could write prose . . . an article on American poetry titled "Advice to the English," notes for the new edition of a textbook.

Pound mentions the London Library. In the Great War T. E. Hulme borrowed some books from the library and took them to the front.

> and a shell buried 'em in a dug-out,
> And the library expressed its annoyance.

There was something admirable about a library that wouldn't accept the Great War as an excuse for not returning books in good condition.

"England expects . . ." The attitude was typical of England as a whole. They weren't in a hurry to be friendly, like the Americans, but once you were a member you had a definite standing and they gave you the benefit of the doubt. You could let a bill go unpaid for three months without getting a nasty letter from the company. But if you turned out to be the kind of person who didn't live up to the trust they had placed in you . . .

I felt a certain guilt for receiving so many benefits and not paying taxes. A strike relieved that feeling: for a week we sat in darkness lighted only by candles and stood in line for candles at a shop down the road. People were cheerful about it, especially the old . . . it was like the blackout during the war. Then everyone had pulled together . . . so different from the

London of today with its teddy boys and wogs, and tourists elbowing you to get on the bus.

That year Oxford University Press published a book of my poems. It was reviewed in the English papers and I was invited to give poetry readings. I read at the poetry society in Earls Court Road and traveled to Manchester and Newcastle. At the Morden Tower in Newcastle the audience came from a bar downstairs and sat around on the floor. It was a nice change from reading at a university.

Once or twice when I gave a poetry reading I was asked why I used colloquial phrases and occasionally a cliché. Apparently they hadn't read Chaucer.

On one occasion I read with an English poet. Before the reading when I talked to him he spoke in a natural, unaffected manner, but when he stood at the lectern he had "an Oxford accent." The English are inherently class-conscious and their poets want to appear well bred. Moreover, they have forgotten or never known how "not to describe but to enact." Most English poems sound like an essay with the addition of meter and rhyme.

I read with Seamus Heaney on Thames Television. Germaine Greer was also on the program. She talked about Sylvia Plath . . . Sylvia was a victim of male chauvinism. This was why she committed suicide.

People were talking about Sylvia Plath, especially in Primrose Hill, for this was where she killed herself, in the house with a plaque stating that Yeats once lived there. Those who had known her dined out on their version of the event. An English critic, A. Alvarez, said that the only kind of poetry that could be taken seriously these days, after concentration camps and the atom bomb, was "extremist," the kind Plath wrote. He placed her with other poets—Robert Lowell was the best known—who wrote directly about their lives and spoke of alcoholism, failed marriages, and insanity.

In the States this kind of writing would be called "confessional." People who didn't like poetry touted confessional writing to the skies—it was a way of denigrating imagination and putting poetry down, making it symptomatic of mental disorder. It was at this time that you began to hear that the future of literature lay in journalism . . . that factual writing was more important than fiction.

I traveled with my wife to Ireland. We stayed with Heaney in Belfast. From there we set out for Derry where I was to give a reading. Seamus was driving . . . he pulled over and stopped. "It's my father," he said. On the far side of a field a man was leaving a pub. Seamus went over and talked to him. He returned to the car. "I haven't seen him in months."

The writing on walls said that Ulster was prepared to fight. We were stopped at a roadblock by British soldiers. They were in Northern Ireland to prevent Irish Catholics and Protestants from killing each other. They made us get out and identify ourselves, and searched the car for weapons.

Seamus left us at the college in Derry and drove back to Belfast. Halfway through my reading a bomb went off in the distance, rattling windows. In a few minutes there was another. The audience didn't turn a hair . . . apparently they were accustomed. This was not being reported in the English papers. They spoke of violence but not that there was practically a civil war in Northern Ireland.

We were driven to the next reading by a man who had been sent to fetch us. The landscape was growing dark and I had an ominous feeling. It took me a while to realize why . . . this was where I had been stationed during the war. We were infantry replacements waiting to be assigned to a regular outfit. We spent our days being instructed in close combat and the use of explosives, skills that would be required in the forthcoming invasion of the Continent. In the evenings we went to Portrush to drink half-and-half in a pub. If anyone had told me that one day I would return to this place of my own free will!

The reading took place at night. The audience sat bolt upright . . . they might have been cased in armor. I read serious poems, humorous poems, and made off-the-cuff remarks, but nothing seemed to work . . . the faces showed no expression. So I did what I had never done before . . . I stopped reading poems and asked what was the matter. What had they expected?

They said that their existence was being threatened by the Catholics. This was what concerned them. Then why, I couldn't help wondering, had they come to hear poems? But we discussed the situation. When I spoke of the shooting of Catholics by the British army on the day that had been named "Black Sunday," a man in the audience corrected me. "We don't call it that," he said, "we call it Good Sunday." I was glad that my wife and I were leaving the next day.

At Seamus's house in Belfast we heard the Catholic side of the story. When he was coming home at night he would be stopped and questioned . . . the ones who questioned him were his neighbors. He was thinking of moving to the Catholic south.

He drove us to the station . . . we were taking the train to Dublin. On the way he handed me a large envelope. It contained a poem he had signed for me as a parting gift. I thanked him, and when we got out of the car I put the envelope in my suitcase.

We approached the entrance to the station. The army was out in force . . . there had been a new wave of bombings. One of the soldiers glancing over the crowd picked out a face that looked suspicious. He stepped in front of me and told me to open the suitcase.

It was full of dirty laundry . . . shirts, underwear, and socks. "What is that?" he said, and pointed to the envelope. I said, "A poem," thinking this would be the end of it. But he tucked the automatic rifle under his arm, reached for the envelope, and took out a sheet of paper. It was what I had always feared, a critic with a gun. But the poem must have been innocent . . . he put it back in the envelope, dropped it in the suitcase, and waved me on.

We told the story when we got back to London, but the people seated at the table were in a hurry to tell an Irish story of their own. The restraint on which English men and women prided themselves was thrown overboard when they spoke of Ireland. A woman who was important in the theater said that the Irish came to England to make good wages and take advantage of the free medical service, and went back to Ireland without paying taxes. Another of the well-bred people at the table said that the Irish used their bathtubs to keep coal in.

BBC television staged a discussion of Ireland as a trial at Bar with three judges seated on the Bench. A rule was laid down at the start: there were to be no references to the past, only to the present trouble. Apparently it had not occurred to anyone at the BBC that British judges in wigs and gowns deciding what to do about Ireland might be a cause of the troubles. Or that in Ireland present and past are inseparable.

To walk on a road in Ireland or sit by the water is to be conscious of the past. These stones are where a monastery used to stand, that field is where the rebels were killed. Their ever-present consciousness of the past makes for poetry . . . the writing of a Yeats, a Patrick Kavanagh, a Seamus Heaney.

We meant to stay for a year . . . we stayed for two. But we had to leave the apartment . . . it was cramped and dark . . . the room where we did most of our living was below street level. We found a house for rent around the corner. It had three floors and light came through the curtains.

The longer we stayed in England the more there was to see. We traveled to Bath to see the Roman ruins and to Stratford to see Peter Brook direct Shakespeare. We went to Richmond to see the palace and Kew to see the flowers. One Sunday we attended a service at Magnus Martyr close by the Thames. As *The Waste Land* said, the walls held "inexplicable splendour of Ionian white and gold."

On another day we were in Little Gidding, and this too was as Eliot described it.

> you leave the rough road
> And turn behind the pig-sty to the dull facade
> And the tombstone.

A visitor's book in the chapel asked you to pray for some who were sick and others who were troubled. Some lines by Eliot were on display to remind you that there are more important things than sightseeing.

You are not here to verify,
Instruct yourself, or inform curiosity
Or carry report. You are here to kneel
Where prayer has been valid.

An appointment book that somehow has survived tells me that I gave a poetry reading at the Hasmonean School; that I saw Ted Hughes and his wife for lunch; that I recorded poems for the Greater London Arts Council; that I had a drink with Derwent May; that I read for "Poetry International" at Queen Elizabeth Hall and at "The Pindar of Wakefield" in Grays Inn Road.

With Daniel Weissbort and Dannie Abse I took part in a "festival of the arts" at the Westminster Synagogue. We were shown the rooms that contained the Sacred Scrolls. There were 1,564 Scrolls, each representing a community in Bohemia or Moravia that had been destroyed by the Germans. But the Germans had preserved the Scrolls, perhaps with a view to having a museum of Jewish life.

In 1964 the Scrolls were brought from Czechoslovakia to London. They were numbered, placed in racks, and repaired so as to be usable. Hundreds of requests for a Scroll had been received from synagogues all over the world. A scribe was sitting at a table repairing a damaged Scroll. He wrote slowly, dipping his pen in ink that had been blessed by a rabbi.

Ron and Fay Weldon lived in the house next door. Fay had written a first novel and was writing another . . . also a script for a television series. She sat in the kitchen over cups of tea, smoking cigarettes. She would get up to attend to one of the children.

I saw Fay recently in New York. She was on a tour arranged by her American publisher to promote her latest novel. We met at a reception being held in her honor at a bar in lower Manhattan. She was about to start on her journey west and looked as if she were being cast adrift. Miriam was with me; she told Fay which of her novels she liked best, and Fay looked surprised . . . you don't expect to meet someone who has actually read your books. She wanted us to stay but we couldn't . . .

we live far out on the Island, a two hours' drive, and had to be starting back.

Fay reminded me that when I was living next door I gave her a bit of advice . . . a talking-to, in fact. I told her that she had introduced too many characters at the beginning of her novel. She confused the reader. I told her she mustn't do it again.

I can see myself talking and Fay listening, her eyes half closed, a curl of smoke going up from the cigarette in her hand. While I am giving her my advice she is thinking how it would sound in the mouth of a character in a novel, a critic. Novelists can find a use for everything . . . even criticism.

Theater Business

"Theatre business, management of men."

—W. B. Yeats

In the summer of 1976 a dean proposed having a Poetry Center and asked if I'd run it. I said yes . . . it seemed like a good idea. I was given a graduate student to assist me and an undergraduate to type letters and make herself generally useful. There would be funds for poetry readings and to buy books and magazines. The Center would be located in a room in the library. In no time at all we had it fixed up with chairs and tables, bookshelves, and poster-size photographs of Walt Whitman and Emily Dickinson.

Our first reader was Richard Wilbur. He would be flying from Connecticut to an airport twenty miles away. I looked for him in the main building but he was not there. This gave me a foretaste of anxieties that were to come: there would be a full auditorium and no poet. But Wilbur appeared, looking unconcerned. The plane had landed in another part of the airport. I drove him to Stony Brook and he gave a masterly performance to a large and enthusiastic audience. The Poetry Center was off to a fine start.

In the years that followed we had readings by other well-known poets at the rate of one a month, with lesser poets between. The Poetry Center was a hive of activity; students came there to read or just to talk. There were readings by Denise Levertov, Lucille Clifton, Robert Bly, Donald Hall and Jane Kenyon, by Seamus Heaney, Robert Duncan, Allen Ginsberg, Gwendolyn Brooks, Czeslaw Milosz, and a dozen others who were famous or trembling on the brink of fame. We also

Ohio Review, no. 44 (1989).

held group readings . . . one by a group of poets from Yugoslavia, another by some French-Canadian poets.

There were readings by younger poets. It was hard to get them an audience. The auditorium would be filled for a poetry reading by Erica Jong, who had made a reputation as a novelist, or for a reading by Robert Lowell, but I couldn't depend on having an audience for some young and comparatively unknown poet, however good the poetry might be.

These readings were open to the public as well as the students and faculty. We sent out flyers and put up posters in local libraries. The Poetry Center had a reputation, even abroad, for we invited foreign poets to read at Stony Brook. If the poet were important enough the university would even pay for a round-trip ticket to the States.

Ted Hughes agreed to come. This made for another kind of anxiety . . . it was rumored that women in the audience would try to disrupt the reading. Ted Hughes had been married to Sylvia Plath and these women said that he was responsible for her committing suicide. They could hardly have known anything about Ted Hughes and Sylvia Plath, but people with an axe to grind don't care whether a story is true or false.

As it turned out, Hughes gave a superb performance and there wasn't a peep from the audience. Most Long Islanders have never been out of the suburbs except for an occasional trip to the city. They were stunned by Ted Hughes's poems about birds and beasts and the sheer bloodiness of nature.

> Nothing but bounce and stab
> And a ravening second.
>
> Is it their single-minded-sized skulls, or a trained
> Body, or genius, or a nestful of brats
> Gives their days this bullet and automatic
> Purpose? Mozart's brain had it, and the shark's mouth
> That hungers down the blood-smell even to a leak of its own
> Side and devouring of itself: efficiency which
> Strikes too streamlined for any doubt to pluck at it
> Or obstruction deflect.

Hughes was accompanied by the British ambassador. The president of the university held a reception in their honor at his house after the reading. The president, J. T., liked our Poetry Center. It can't be much fun being a president . . . eveyone wants something from you, and they resent it when you refuse. I used to hear a good deal of murmuring against the president behind his back. He'd refused a dean the funds he requested for a pet project; a department had voted to grant one of its members tenure, and J. T. had vetoed it on the ground that the man wasn't qualified.

But he supported the Poetry Center. What's more, he came to the readings. Anyone who knows anything about universities will know how remarkable this is. Whatever university presidents may have stood for in the past, today they are in the business of fund-raising. Therefore they favor the sciences and social sciences. An oil company may be persuaded to subsidize the new "earth science" building, or a business to pay for experiments in psychology that will result in new kinds of advertising. But no one gives money for the humanities. A university president who goes to poetry readings is an anomaly indeed.

We filmed the poetry readings. Today if you visit the library at Stony Brook you may look at moving pictures of poets reading aloud for fifty minutes or half an hour. Now and then the film jags and the camera swings back to focus on the top of the poet's head or his Adam's apple. One of the burdens under which art labors in a state system is that it has to be educational, and we had to train students as cameramen . . . the university let us have the cameras on this condition.

Poetry is not one of the performing arts. Some poets, however, tried to make it so: they got themselves up in costume; they mugged for the camera; they crouched down behind the lectern and shot up again. I was told that one poet's lecture agent guaranteed that at a certain moment in the reading she would cry.

I ran the Poetry Center in addition to my teaching. If asked why, I would say that I wanted to make life at the university more interesting. I wasn't being paid for overtime . . . in fact, the receptions I gave at my house for the poets, students, and anyone else who wanted to come, were costing me money. There was a more serious consideration . . . what with seeing that the poets arrived on time, introducing them on the platform, entertaining them, and putting them to bed, I wasn't getting much writing done.

In the summer of 1978 we held a "British-American Poetry Festival." I forget whose idea it was . . . probably mine. We invited six British poets . . . in addition to a handsome fee we would pay their way across the Atlantic and back. They were Geoffrey Hill, Elaine Feinstein, Fleur Adcock, Patricia Beer, Tony Harrison, and Adrian Mitchell. The American poets were Alice Walker, Donald Hall, Stanley Plumly, Al Young, Judith Johnson Sherwin, and Galway Kinnell. To ensure having a knowledgeable audience we invited a number of other poets just to attend, and we hoped they would take part in the panel discussions. We couldn't pay them a fee but we paid for their transportation and offered to house and feed them.

The university put up $12,000 for the festival, and a woman I knew, a patron of the arts, gave another $5,000.

Three weeks before the festival was scheduled to start, an official at the headquarters of the State University, located in Albany, stopped the funds. He was reported to have said, "What is a poetry festival? A social occasion?" I was informed of this on a Friday and spent the next forty-eight hours thinking about it. The poets had agreed to come on my say-so . . . six of them from England. They had put aside the time and refused other engagements. I was personally responsible . . . they had agreed to come because they knew me or knew who I was.

In the days that followed, the obstacle in Albany was persuaded to give way. But I had arrived at a decision. It was clear that I couldn't rely on the promises of the people who ran the university . . . you had to have everything in writing. If you wanted to do anything for the university, anything excellent and unusual, you would have to argue, cajole, and plead. You would have to give all your time to it . . . in short, become one of them.

Creating "an audience for art" is one of the temptations artists face. When you aren't able to work you become an administrator.

This matter of the withheld funds gave me an excuse for leaving the Poetry Center. I had been wanting to leave for some time—I was finding "theater business" irksome. In general, poets were better on the page than they were in person. Their lines breathed compassion—in person they could be vain and calculating. Some of them lost all restraint when there was an audience and the opportunity to shine.

One night two poets tossed a coin to decide who would read first, who second. Some poets cared a great deal about this—the second reader would be the one whose voice the audience carried with them as they left. A few minutes before the first reader was to go on he drew me aside and said that if he wasn't put on second he wouldn't read at all. My impulse was to tell him to go to hell, but the other reader said that he didn't mind and let him have his way.

I once took part in a group reading in New York City that was held to publicize a little magazine. A number of writers had agreed to read for no more than ten minutes each so that everyone would have equal time. When it came the turn of a novelist to mount the platform he couldn't be found. He appeared at the end of the evening, saying that he'd been delayed in traffic. So he was put on last. He read a few pages of a scene. His time was up but he continued to read, and the people in charge did nothing. The he said he had a somewhat longer piece . . . should he read it or not? No one shouted "Not," and he stretched his ten minutes to half an hour. It was a superb example of hogsmanship, and I recommend it to all schools where they teach "creative writing," for writing is only part of the craft . . . there is also making a name and getting ahead.

The British-American Poetry Festival took place over three days in July. It was beautiful weather, the landscape lush and green as it is in the summer in Suffolk County. The poets wandered around chatting happily between readings and panel discussions. We fed them three times a day . . . this was one of our mistakes. Forty places were set for breakfast, costing a pretty penny at the caterer's, and only two or three guests showed up. The rest were in bed nursing a hangover.

The festival was a success. Years later I met one of the British poets at another festival, in Toronto, and she spoke fondly of her time at Stony Brook.

This was my last act as director. After I left, the Center was broken up. The books were sent downstairs to another part of the library and shelved in a corner. The room was reclaimed by an administrator . . . it was in his territory and he'd come to regret letting us use it. There was too much coming and going in the Poetry Center. Sometimes there would be sounds of laughter.

The last time I looked in, the room was being used to store office furniture. Chairs were piled on desks. The big photographs of Walt Whitman and Emily Dickinson had been taken down.

Schloimy Goes to the Post Office

The new issue of *Midtown* arrives. I open it to the table of contents and there's my poem.

But what's this? Schloimy has a poem in the same issue, right up front. His writing manages to be at once obscene and boring, and in person he's detestable. He peers at you through thick glasses with an arrogant expression. He made a reputation when he was young for iconoclasm: he insulted older writers. Now he's an icon himself and a pillar of the Establishment. He wears a tie and goes to receptions "hosted" by rich people. It's evident that all Schloimy wanted from the start was to change places with the people he was insulting: to sit on the committees that award prizes; to have his picture on the society page of the *Times* with other patrons of the arts who are talking to a Russian poet.

And here's my name, separated from his, my thoughts separated from his, by only a few pages of printed matter.

"I'm never going to send *Midtown* anything again," I tell my wife. "They have no standards at all. There's a poem by Schloimy on page eight."

She says, "Schloimy goes to the post office. Does that mean you'll never go?"

Where else does Schloimy go? To the supermarket and to a store to buy clothes. He goes to a dentist, to the movies. In July he goes to the beach. He has been to London, Paris, and Rome. Two years ago he traveled in Russia, and now, says the note in *Midtown,* he is planning a trip to China. Everywhere

---

From "Entries" in "Work-in-Progress," ed. M. L. Rosenthal, *Ploughshares*, Spring 1991.

you think of going, Schloimy has been. Does this mean you're never to go anywhere?

And it's not just where he goes but what he does. He gets up in the morning and puts on pants and a shirt. He has breakfast . . . then, I suppose, he works. Between twelve and two he has lunch. Maybe a little snooze. In the afternoon he goes for a walk. He eats dinner, watches TV, sleeps. For all you know, though it's unlikely, he may have a girl friend or even be married. It's just barely possible. Does this mean you are never to have sexual relations?

My wife's question has given me a way of solving troublesome questions, matters of conscience. There are Schloimys all over the world doing the things I do or think of doing. Schloimy eats and drinks. Should I therefore starve or die of thirst? Schloimy breathes . . . should I give up breathing? It is clear that if I want to live I must live in the same world as Schloimy.

In the life after death, assuming there is one, who's that walking in front of me? Talking to St. Peter at the gate? You guessed it . . . who but Schloimy. He's being admitted—St. Peter, it seems, is no wiser than the members of the academies and institutes of this world to which Schloimy belonged. There he goes, with his bald head and stoop, to pay his respects and take a seat among the members. Schloimy as an angel in heaven . . .

Does this mean I must retrace my steps and go in the opposite direction?

Entries

To Whom Can I Speak Today?

To whom can I speak today?
  One's fellows are evil;
  The friends of today do not love.
To whom can I speak today?
  Faces have disappeared:
  Every man has a downcast face toward his fellow.
To whom can I speak today?
  A man should arouse wrath by his evil character,
  But he stirs everyone to laughter, in spite of
    the wickedness of his sin.
To whom can I speak today?
  There is no righteous;
  The land is left to those who do wrong.
To whom can I speak today?
  The sin that afflicts the land,
  It has no end.

> "Dispute of a Man, Who Contemplates
> Suicide, with His Soul." Egypt, c. 2000 B.C.

The poem is cited by Eric Voegelin in *Order and History,* volume 1. Voegelin comments: "The fellow man casts down his eyes so that you will not read in them the deal he has made with evil and know that he has become a conniver."

From "Works-in-Progress," ed. M. L. Rosenthal, *Ploughshares,* Spring 1991.

"The age demanded . . ."

I had written a book of poems, and on Fifth Avenue, at
Barnes and Noble, they were selling
   The Passion and the Rage by Elizabeth Godwin. "Theirs was a
love scorched by treason and dangerous destiny . . ."
   Love's Sweet Agony by Patricia Matthews. "A sensational new
novel by America's first lady of historical romance."
   Sweet Abandon by Wendy Lozano. "He turned her vows of
purity into the fires of love!"

Auden's Touchstone

> "All bad poetry comes from genuine feeling," he says, as Au-
> den would say after him.
>
> Richard Ellmann, *Oscar Wilde*

Auden's true ancestor was Oscar Wilde, though I don't recall
his saying so.
   Auden says that, like Matthew Arnold, he has his touch-
stones, "but they are for testing critics, not poets." There are
four questions he would ask a critic.

> "Do you like, and by like I really mean like, not approve of on
> principle:
>
> 1) Long lists of proper names such as the Old Testament
>   genealogies or the Catalogue of ships in the *Iliad*?
> 2) Riddles and all other ways of not calling a spade a
>   spade?
> 3) Complicated verse forms of great technical difficulty,
>   such as Englyns, Drott-Kvaetts, Sestinas, even if their
>   content is trivial?
> 4) Conscious theatrical exaggeration, pieces of Baroque flat-
>   tery, like Dryden's welcome to the Duchess of Ormond?"

If a critic could truthfully answer "yes" to all four, then I
should trust his judgment implicitly on all literary matters.

This is from an Inaugural Lecture Auden delivered at the University of Oxford on June 11, 1956. I imagine it went over well with that audience. All these questions were one: "Do you like, and by like I really mean like, camp? If so I shall trust your judgment implicitly on all literary matters."

Willows

... "inspiration" may ... refer to the inducement of the ... poetic condition by the act of listening to the wind, the messenger of the Goddess Cardea, in a sacred grove.

Mount Helicon ... took its name as much from helicë, the willow-tree sacred to poets, as from the stream which spiralled round it.

Robert Graves, *The White Goddess*

When I was a schoolboy I used to read a book beneath the willows that lined the road from the gate to the chapel. They were always swaying and whispering. One of the first poems I published was about the willows ... I compared them to women. I had no idea that the willow was sacred to poets, or that listening to the wind inspired "the poetic condition," or that those whom Graves calls "true poets" are lovers of women. Apparently Graves is right: there is a poetic character and poets have the same kinds of experience.

On Originality

The pursuit of novelty and originality is a false need that poorly conceals banality or lack of temperament.

Paul Cézanne

Some centuries presume to remake everything in the arts and other disciplines because they themselves do not know how to make anything.

Giacomo Leopardi

Postmodernism: An Afterthought

I received a notice of a panel discussion under the auspices of the Poetry Project to be held at St. Mark's Church in Manhattan. The topic to be discussed was "What Happens after Post-Modernism?" The organizers acknowledged "generous support" from certain public and private agencies: the New York Council on the Arts, the New York Council for the Humanities, the National Endowment for the Arts.

These are very generous agencies indeed, considering the vagueness of the topic under discussion. While the avant-garde—in this instance the avant-avant-garde—is discussing what happens after Postmodernism, for many of us it has not yet arrived. No one seems to know what it is, and you will have a hard time finding out. Consider, for example, the following passage from an article on Postmodernism by Marc J. Bensimon:

> Like Baudrillard, Michel Serres's "La Thanatocratie" (1974) denounces a modern world destined for its own self-destruction. Indetermination (simulation and phantasy of determination) is for Serres over-determination, but he has the same vision of an irreversible drive. A "death instinct" prepares for humanity, with the help of industry, science, and strategy, a genocide from which perverse enjoyment is not excluded.[1]

This is typical of the dismal verbiage that poured out of Paris in the 1970s and 1980s and has been accepted as gospel by American academics.

A more understandable explanation is offered by Ihab Hassan.[2] He too talks in abstractions, but when he lines them up in parallel columns we see what he means. I can't reproduce the columns here in their entirety, but enough to give an idea.

---

1. Marc J. Bensimon, "Apocalypse Now or in the Magic Hole," in *Modernism: Challenges and Perspectives,* ed. Monique Chefdor, Ricardo Quinones, and Albert Wachtel (Urbana, Ill.: University of Illinois Press, 1986), p. 291.

2. Ihab Hassan, "The Culture of Postmodernism," in *Modernism: Challenges and Perspectives,* p. 312.

The left column is headed Modernism, the right Postmodernism. Under Modernism he lists:

Romanticism/Symbolism
Form (conjunctive, closed)
Purpose
Design
Hierarchy

Under Postmodernism:

Pataphysics/Dadaism
Play
Chance
Anarchy

The word Pataphysics, in case we aren't all up on our jargon, is taken from a novel by Alfred Jarry in which things are described as they appear to be rather than as reason tells us they are.

Continuing down the columns, under Modernism we find:

Mastery/Logos
Art Object/Finished Work
Distance
Creation/Totalization/Synthesis

In the opposite column, Postmodernism:

Exhaustion/Silence
Process/Performance/Happening
Decreation/Deconstruction/Antithesis

Near the bottom of the columns we come to the nitty-gritty: under Modernism, God the Father. Under Postmodernism, the Holy Ghost.

The principle on which Hassan divides Postmodernist sheep from Modernist goats is quite simple. For all the words listed under Modernism you may substitute one word, Author. For all the words under Postmodernism, substitute Theorist. It is the author who believes in Form and Purpose and Design, the theoriest who argues for Antiform (thereby being rid of the obligation to make sense). It is the author who believes in Finished Work and the theoriest who prefers Performance and Happening. It is the author who works like God to make something, and the theorist who is filled with the Holy Ghost, that is, with words.

The Modernist creates works that strike us as being true by reason of their perfection. The striving for perfection implies there is an order outside life, a form of truth and beauty that the artist has envisioned and is striving to show.

The Postmodernist, on the other hand, assumes that society is the only reality and there is nothing beyond language, no "truth" to which language refers. (Postmodernists always put the word truth in quotes.) "For structuralism in general," says the Marxist critic Jameson, "there has been a tendency to feel that reference is a kind of myth, that one can no longer talk about the 'real' in that external objective way."[3]

As there are no external referents, no "truth," it follows that words mean whatever we want them to mean. Therefore the proper study of mankind and womankind is rhetoric, the art of persuading others, and the best rhetorician is the best philosopher. As Humpty Dumpty said when Alice wondered if you could make words mean so many different things, "The question is, which is to be master, that's all."

So, in answer to the question, "What Happens After Postmodernism?," it is clear that in the place of art we shall have politics, until it comes out of our ears.

An Affluent Society

We suffer now the sores of long peace. Crueller than arms
Luxury has set in, avenging the conquered globe.

---

3. Frederic Jameson, "Postmodernism and Consumer Society," in *The Anti-Aesthetic: Essays on Postmodern Culture,* ed. Hal Foster (Seattle: Bay Press, 1983), p. 119.

Not one crime has been wanting or one act of lust
Since Roman poverty expired.

> Juvenal, "Satire VI," trans. Steven Robinson

Social Justice

Among the inexorable questions of human existence is that of
social justice. It is one, undoubtedly; but also undoubtedly, it is
only one.

> Ortega y Gasset, *Man and Crisis*

Ortega asks, "Suppose some despairing men resolve that
there is no question other than this, or that this at least is the
decisive question . . . the only one which ought to occupy us;
and that all the rest ought to be subordinated to it." Well, this
is what has been happening throughout the century; we have
been compelled by those who are obsessed with social justice
to drop everything and think of social justice, to struggle and
die around it. We must give our lives to this or perish. The
individual is compelled to think as the crowd thinks, and the
crowd's idea of social justice is that held by its leaders. "Peri-
ods of desperation open a wide field for all personal fictions."
The fictions of a Stalin, a Hitler, a Mao Tse-tung, become
social justice.

The Leech-Gatherer

When Wm. and I returned from accompanying Jones, we
met an old man almost double. He had on a coat, thrown
over his shoulders, above his waistcoat and coat. Under this
he carried a bundle, and had an apron on and a night-cap.
His face was interesting. He had dark eyes and a long nose.
John, who afterwards met him at Wytheburn, took him for a
Jew. He was of Scotch parents, but had been born in the
army. He had had a wife, and "a good woman, and it
pleased God to bless us with ten children." All these were
dead but one, of whom he had not heard for many years, a
sailor. His trade was to gather leeches, but now leeches are

scarce, and he had not strength for it. He lived by begging, and was making his way to Carlisle, where he should buy a few godly books to sell. He said leeches were very scarce, partly owing to this dry season, but many years they have been scarce—he supposed it owing to their being much sought after, that they did not breed fast, and were of slow growth. Leeches were formerly 2s. 6d. [per] 100; they are now 30s. He had been hurt in driving a cart, his leg broke, his body driven over, his skull fractured. He felt no pain till he recovered from his first insensibility. It was then late in the evening, when the light was just going away.

Dorothy Wordsworth, *Journals*

The Sister's Version

And it pleased God to bless them
with ten children, all of whom
are dead but one, a sailor.

His trade is gathering leeches
but he no longer has the strength.
For years they have been scarce.

So now he lives by begging,
and is making his way to Carlisle
to buy a few godly books to sell.

He was hurt driving a cart . . .
his leg broken, his body
driven over. He felt no pain at first.

Her eyes are fastened on his
as he speaks. She is listening
in an agony of attention.

Dorothy heard the old man say that he lived by begging—a point ignored by Wordsworth when he titled his poem "Resolution and Independence." He was hearing the sound of the old man's voice rather than what it said.

But now his voice to me was like a stream
Scarce heard; nor word from word could I divide . . .

When Dorothy was hearing the old man say that once he'd been run over driving a cart and his leg broken, Wordsworth was imagining

> a sea-beast crawled forth, that on a shelf
> Of rock or sand reposeth, there to sun itself.

Wordsworth says that talking to the leech-gatherer relieved his anxiety about the future: if the old man could keep body and soul together by gathering leeches, and have so calm a mind, then he could laugh at his own fears. But it was not the old man's example that restored Wordsworth's confidence—it was the return of visionary power . . . imagination. The poet need not worry about Providence—he *is* Providence.

A Gift[4]

Molière wrote, "Anyone may be an honorable man and yet write verse badly." This was in the 17th century, before Michael Newman's Verse Perfect poetry processor. Using Mr. Newman's software for MSDOS computers, anyone, honorable or not, can harness the algorithmic powers of the micro-processor to generate acceptable verse in forms ranging from iambic-pentameter sonnets to rap music lyrics. . . .

The Poetry Processor . . . automates the mechanics of poetry, freeing the writer to concentrate on thought and emotion. The user creates the poem on one side of the screen, while on the other the computer keeps track of meter and rhyme. Even the rhyming can be automated; place the censor on a word and press a key to see a list of rhyming words. . . .

> Peter H. Lewis, "A Touch of the Poet,"
> *New York Times: Education Life,*
> August 6, 1989

---

4.   "Let me disclose the gifts reserved for age. . . .
    . . . the conscious impotence of rage
      At human folly, and the laceration
      Of laughter at what ceases to amuse."
                    T. S. Eliot, *Four Quartets*

On Education

Mencken on the University

. . . first the typical American university president, a jenkins to wealth, an ignominious waiter in ante-chambers and puller of wires, a politician, a fraud and a cad; and secondly, the typical American professor, a puerile and pitiable slave.

Prejudices: Fifth Series

"The people we appoint to educate"

We can be sure that most of the people we appoint to educate our children have not been educated. Yet we assume that they can give something that they themselves have not received, and that this is the only way one can get an education.

Giacomo Leopardi, *Pensieri*

Allan Bloom on the University

. . . an unsatisfactory halfway house between the two harsh disciplines that make a man serious—community and solitude.

The Closing of the American Mind

Last But Not Least

. . . the power of instruction is seldom of much efficacy, except in those happy dispositions where it is almost superfluous.

Edward Gibbon

Academic Prose

Elizabeth and Darcy are more complex and mixed figures than these more simple types; each both maintains ideals and is motivated economically and passionately. Each both reads books and goes to balls.

Richard Eldridge, *On Moral Personhood*

A Professor of Communications

"A fear of snakes or of dentists are rare events, and they're easy to avoid, and yet communicating with people comes up all the time," said Michael J. Beatty, a professor of communications at Cleveland State University.

New York Times, May 29, 1989

Could We Have That Again, Please?

Her retellings of myth would be reverent (in their inquiry into the psychic reality of such immemorial stories) were they not so irreverent.

Helen Vendler, New Yorker, July 27, 1987

"Because of transgressions and in lieu of performance," he said just before the end of the season, "there will be some changes in protocol."

Davey Johnson, manager of the Mets, quoted in New York Times, October 25, 1989

Whitman stands with one foot firmly entrenched in the romantic tradition while he steps boldly with the other towards modernism.

A student, December 1989

"Poetry is . . ." (Mencken)

Poetry is the product of an effort to invent a world appreciably better than the one we live in; its essence is not the representation of the facts, but the deliberate concealment and denial of the facts.

Mencken, Prejudices: Third Series

One of Hemingway's characters remarks that Mencken has said everything he knows about the things he knows something about and now he is onto the things he knows nothing about. Mencken is splendid on William Jennings Bryan—"He liked the heavy, greasy victuals of the farmhouse kitchen"— but it is clear from his description of poetry that he doesn't understand it. "Denial of the facts" is what the boobs Mencken held up to ridicule take poetry to be. In this he is like that other good writer of prose, Edmund Wilson. Both Mencken and Wilson relegated poetry to the role prescribed for it by Mallarmé in the 1880s: poetry is too fine for this world. In so doing they reserved to prose and to themselves all seriousness and truth.

Curiously, in the same book in which he describes poetry as nonsense, Mencken points another, very different direction poetry was to take in this century. "Accurate representation," he writes, "is not . . . inimical to beauty . . . the most careful and penetrating representation is itself the source of a rare and wonderful beauty."

> Flowers through the window
> lavender and yellow
> changed by white curtains—
> Smell of cleanliness—
>
> Sunshine of late afternoon—
> On the glass tray
>
> a glass pitcher, the tumbler
> turned down, by which
>
> a key is lying—And the
> immaculate white bed
>   William Carlos Williams, "Nantucket"

Williams's originality lay in his making poetry of the least poetic-seeming objects and incidents. The tediousness of life in Rutherford forced him to dwell with an almost painful intensity on the things chance brought to his attention: a broken bottle, the severed head of a cod rising and falling under water, an old woman in the street eating plums out of a paper bag. "If the fool would persist in his folly he would become wise," said William Blake, and in this instance he appears to have been right. Williams's poems show American streets and lives, the things we have around us, in a clear light. At times the intensity of his looking almost charges the object with significance. We seem to be trembling on the brink of a revelation. It doesn't come, but we keep hoping that it may.

A Lovable Writer

The truth is, he cannot have been in any very high degree ambitious; he was not an abundant producer, and there was manifest a strain of generous indolence in his composition. There was a lovable want of eagerness about him.

Henry James on Hawthorne

The Human Race Degraded

Primo Levi survived a German concentration camp and wrote about the experience . . . "without self-indulgence" says the introduction to my copy of *If This Is a Man*. "There isn't even a hint of hysterical recrimination." Yet, forty-two years later he killed himself. I think the reason is in these words coming toward the end of the book: "The experience of someone who has lived for days during which man was merely a thing in the eyes of man is non-human."

Levi lived many such days in Auschwitz. For days, weeks, and months he was "merely a thing in the eyes of man." After he was liberated he lived again like a human being and wrote his books. But there was a part of his mind that remained behind barbed wire—one does not recover from such experiences.

To have been in Auschwitz is to bear for the rest of one's life a prisoner's number stamped on one's heart. It is to be humiliated and beaten, to be forced to labor in the cold, reduced to stealing and scheming in order to obtain a few mouthfuls of soup. And always with the knowledge that tomorrow you may be sent to the gas chamber.

The Germans did not merely torture and kill millions of people . . . they degraded the human race by showing to what depths of cruelty it might sink. Auschwitz makes you despair of the human race. When the memory comes flooding back it could make you sick of life . . . so sick that you throw yourself down the stairs.

Così Fan Tutti

As for what he did, how can any of us know what we would
have done under those same circumstances?

> James Atlas, on Paul de Man's writing
> for *Le Soir,* a pro-Nazi newspaper

Inner Bodies

Harcourt Brace Jovanovich congratulates Mary McCarthy on
her election to the American Academy of Arts and Letters, the
fifty-member inner body of the American Academy and Insti-
tute of Arts and Letters.

> —Advertisement in the *New York Times,* May 18, 1989

So that inner body, the American Academy and Institute of
Arts and Letters, has an inner body. And if you unscrewed it,
would that have an inner body?

William James, while on a trip to Europe, was elected to
the American Academy of Arts and Letters. On his return
he wrote to the Academy secretary as follows, tendering his
resignation.

> I am not informed that this Academy has any very definite
> work cut out for it of the sort in which I could bear a useful
> part; and it suggests *tant soit peu* the notion of an organization
> for the mere purpose of distinguishing certain individuals
> (with their own connivance) and enabling them to say to the
> world at large "we are in and you are out."

On Modesty

If an artist, scientist, or intellectual of whatever discipline is in
the habit of comparing himself not to other members of his
discipline but rather to the discipline itself, then the more intel-
ligent he is the lower will be his opinion of himself. For his
sense of his own inferiority grows in direct proportion to his

deepening knowledge of his discipline. This is why all great men are modest. . . .

Giacomo Leopardi, *Pensieri*

But Will They Understand?

Live like a bourgeois and think like a god.

Flaubert

Lausa la mare e tente 'n terro. (Praise the sea and stay on land.)

Provençal saying

A Walk with Bashō

Three hundred years ago the Japanese poet Bashō wrote a book about setting out on foot on *The Narrow Road to the Deep North*. He wrote about the scenery, people he met, roadside shrines, places that told a story. Now and then he would write a haiku, a poem in the five-seven-five syllable form. I have thought of setting out on foot across Long Island, but for the present am content to walk with my wife and our dogs on the road to the shore, then around to the mouth of the harbor, and back through the woods.

It is only a five-minute walk from our house to the water. At low tide you can see planks covered with mud, all that's left of a sailing ship that drifted here and was abandoned. I imagine Bashō would have written one of his little Buddhistic poems about it.

> Old boards by the sea
> when the tide runs around them
> still long to sail free.

There is a small harbor, in July and August filled with motorboats, an earsplitting racket. There are even people on water scooters, darting in and out. The beach is littered with seat cushions, plastic containers, bottles . . . anything that can fall or be thrown from a boat. As we walk Miriam and I pick up the pieces of broken glass and put them in a bag. When we started doing this we thought it futile—we would never be able to pick up all the glass. But in fact we have managed to

New England Review, Summer 1992.

do so, for we take this walk every day if it isn't actually raining or snowing.

As you follow the shore around, Port Jefferson's harbor opens before you. In the War of 1812 two British warships entered the harbor and captured seven merchantmen. There was a cannon here on the point . . . some American patriots fired it at the British. The balls went skipping and sank, and in the excitement one of the merchantmen ran aground. Subsequently the British returned the other vessels to their owners, for a price.

Every American wasn't so patriotic. There was as much disagreement about the War of Independence and the War of 1812 as there is about our wars today. We speak of history as though everyone was for it, but there were people in this part of Long Island, Tories, who hated the revolution. Some of them left the country when history won.

Port Jefferson has a striking landmark . . . three chimneys. How often I've tried to write about them as they deserve! They are like three sisters, two tall and slender, one shorter by a head and shoulders. She's the one who stays home and does the ironing while her more favored sisters are at the ball. When she has finished ironing, she sews . . . no, these nights she watches television. But since I'm imagining, why not let her read? She sits by the window reading a novel and glancing now and then at the moon above the trees.

> The moon bright and round
> troubles my heart. The old pond
> frog-jumping-in sound.

Behind the waterfront with its ferry building and restaurants lies the life of a small town. In summer Port Jefferson is a resort for tourists who come over on the ferry from Connecticut. Twenty years ago the streets were deserted . . . they gave that impression. But now they are lined with shops that sell macramé and scented candles, T-shirts, antiques . . . everything to appeal to the stranger whose money is burning a hole in her purse.

Following the shore we pass a grassy area that serves the

village as a park. Every year someone puts a notice in our mailbox announcing that there is to be an ANNUAL FAMILY PICNIC. There will be a Biathlon and Kids' Games (3 Leg, Water Balloon, Wheelbarrow, Sack). Adult Eggtoss LAST. At 5:00 there will be Food & Goodies, and AFTER, Music and Dancing. Miriam and I have never attended one of these family picnics. The little patch of weeds that calls itself a park has an ordinance against dogs. I once tried walking Willa and Custis Lee across a corner to get to the beach, and was confronted by a phalanx of citizens . . . they wouldn't let us cross. So they can keep their kids' games and adult games.

Life in our village isn't all sweetness and light, music and dancing. A friend once told me, "You have to choose . . . either people or trees." We have the trees . . . people you can be friendly with are harder to find, and some are downright unfriendly.

We walk back through the woods. They are being cut down to make way for houses. There used to be acres of trees . . . and brambles. I have been caught in the brambles, looking for Willa. She is a beagle, and cold weather brings out her hunting side—it's impossible to fence her in. I have stood in the middle of the wood on a winter's night calling her name and struggling with a thorn bush, the moon gazing down on my predicament.

> She's hot on the trail.
> I am caught in a thorn bush.
> Ridiculous male!

II

Ships Going into the Blue

A Window

. . . life is much more successfully looked at from a single window, after all.

The Great Gatsby

Breezy and cold, a sun like a diamond blazing so that you can't look at it . . . the trees and hedge in front of my window are dark shapes. When I think that every day of my life I look at the sky and earth directly, it's a blessing.

It says to me, Write! But it doesn't say what about. That is where nature leaves off, cuts the towline . . . where work starts and those who can't do it fall astern. Up ahead are the great ships going into the blue.

Miriam comes back from the walk she takes every afternoon and stops by my study to press her face to the glass and make a mouth like a goldfish. These are the whims that make life worth living. There are people who know this, and then there are the others who provide us with our daily quota of bad news.

Aristotle said that humanity is the animal that lives in a *polis*. How about, the animal that makes faces?

Platero and I

The translator of *Platero and I,* Antonio T. de Nicolás, is himself a poet and philosopher. As he tells us in his "Afterthoughts," when he was a child he too lived in Castillian Spain, the setting of this story. Like Juan Ramón Jiménez, de Nicolás believes that poetry is heard in solitude and silence. In the United States, where silence is frequently interrupted, he lives in what he calls the "forest." The landscape of his childhood was mountainous and spare, with hidden streams and flowering meadows in which pine groves would offer shade from the sun. The "forest" is a place of lanes overhung with trees; in summer the houses are almost hidden in thick, green foliage. The spare, sculptured landscape of Castile and the "forest" of Long Island, "the old island here that flowered once for Dutch sailors' eyes—a fresh green breast of the new world," so an American writer describes it—these landscapes, seemingly so unlike, are joined in the imagination of de Nicolás as places fit, indeed eminently favorable, to the process of silence and meditation out of which paired butterflies float, writing dark lines in the air.

I finished reading his translation on a train that was carrying me late at night away from Manhattan, the most advanced city of industrial commercialized man, back to the forest where, like de Nicolás, I strive to see what the butterflies are writing. I read to the end with growing apprehension, for I knew what was coming: stories about animals always end unhappily. Or so I thought until I actually reached the end,

---

Introduction to *Platero and I,* by Juan Ramón Jiménez (New York: Paragon House, 1986).

where Platero is transfigured. In the page titled "Nostalgia" Platero is lifted above the earth to some place from where he sees men and women, children, beasts, flowers, trees, and streams he once knew. He is looking down with infinite tenderness. This is far from the irony that sees the world as a comedy, irony acting as a shield against the pain of death and loss. Far too from pity that distances the observer. Here, on the contrary, there is acceptance of what happens, joy or pain. Platero wishes only to live, enjoying everything gaily; the taste of a pomegranate, the yellow lilies and singing orioles in the orchard of La Piña where he is buried. Before such love the mental barrier we think of as death must fall. The love given by Platero and the love he inspired in the hearts of others continue to exist. There is no dying, no separation of earth and sky, only existence, which is expressed in words. As another great poet has said:

> Perhaps we are *here* in order to say: house,
> bridge, fountain, gate, pitcher, fruit-tree, window . . .

On the train back to the forest, as buildings and houses went sliding by in a night lit not with stars but electricity, I felt that this book by Juan Ramón Jiménez had accomplished a wonderful thing: it made love a physical reality. The world conspires to make us think that love is only an idea; sometimes it tries to persuade us that love is a fiction, and when we are despondent we may believe that it is. But in reading these pages I was aware of a space beneath the heart and about the size of a walnut that vibrated to the words on the page, a nucleus of intense feeling. To say that I felt happy or sad would have been beside the point. There was a life that could be felt when words such as these were read, a life stronger than the walls and shedding a more dazzling light than the electric signboards in the night of Long Island.

The nucleus, life, is open to the earth and sky, whatever one sees. Some things are terrible to see. A mangy dog, thin and panting, wanders around. One day a guard, for no reason, shoots the wretched creature. "A veil appeared to dress the sun in mourning." Yes, that would be so. "Platero stared at the dog, head high," and the dog Diana, Platero's companion, "walked about from one to the other trying to hide." So do we all, in this terrible century, wish to hide—this century of murders for no reason. But what joy there is in living, all the same! A canary flies out of its cage and flies about the orchard, in the pine, the lilacs. In the evening he comes back to the house and "without anyone knowing how or why, he appeared in his cage, joyful again. What excitement in the garden! The children jumped, clapping hands, flushed and laughing like the dawn; Diana, crazy, ran after them, barking at her own laughing tiny bells."

Platero witnesses and shares in everything. He is joyfully alive in the words, the living flesh, of his book.

Life with the Real White Goddess

"What a set! What a world!" Matthew Arnold exclaimed after reading an account of Shelley's private life. What would he have said of the private life of Robert Graves and Laura Riding as described by Graves's nephew Richard in his biography of the poet? Robert, his wife, Nancy, and Laura lived in a *ménage à trois*, then in a "four-life" with the poet Geoffrey Phibbs. They were "united in adopting a new scale of values, according to which certain actions which were then normally considered to be grossly unprincipled became highly commendable."

The actions and private conversations are here reported in detail, sometimes from day to day, as though the biographer were standing outside the door taking notes. He may have known people who knew Robert Graves and Laura Riding, but the main source appears to have been "the vast collection of family papers built up by Robert Graves's brother John Graves. (1903–80) and now owned by John's son Richard, the present author." Other collections of letters and papers have been consulted. The biography is authoritative, yet as lively as a novel in its recording of the flux of emotions and the behavior of Laura Riding's inner circle. It was she, the obscure poet, who set the "new scale of values." Graves, who would be far better known as a poet, the author of a controversial autobiography, *Good-bye to All That,* and a best-selling novel, *I, Claudius,* stood in awe of her.

The private life of Robert Graves and Laura Riding is not only interesting in itself; it is important to the history of litera-

---

Review of Richard Perceval Graves, *Robert Graves: The Years with Laura, 1926–40, New York Times Book Review,* November 11, 1990.

ture, for the life fed directly into the writing. A case in point: no work on poetry has been more influential than *The White Goddess,* Graves's study of mythology in its connections with poetry; dozens of poets and professors have gained a reputation for originality by stealing from it. If we look into this biography we see that the goddess is very similar to Laura Riding and demands the same kind of service from her followers that she demanded of Robert. The goddess "worships the male infant, not the grown man: it is evidence of her deity, of man's dependence on her life." From the biography we learn how dependent Robert was on Laura—he had come out of the Great War with shattered nerves and marriage to a woman he did not love. When Laura Riding appeared he handed over the direction of his life and work to her—a dependence he would later come to regret.

In *The White Goddess* we read that the male gods Osiris and Set compete for the favor of the female, Isis. "She tries to satisfy both, but can only do so by alternate murder, and man tries to regard this as evidence of her fundamental falsity, not of his own irreconcilable demands on her." (The irreconcilable demands are that she should be a goddess and at the same time behave as an ordinary woman.) In the biography we read: "Despite Graves's obvious devotion to Riding, she now began to show an interest in other men which, though it did not lead to sexual intercourse . . . was undoubtedly based upon strong sexual attraction. Graves at once became subject to a new set of intensely emotional pressures, and began to depict himself in an unnaturally humble manner, condemning (for example) what he saw as his 'greed and credulity'; and imagining himself, when retelling the legend of Isis, not as Set, her new young lover, but as 'Osiris yearly drowned.' "

Graves was the supplicant, Laura Riding the embodiment of the goddess and dispenser of favors. When she decided that sexual intercourse was dirty and unnecessary, he agreed to give up sex. Even after he had been replaced in her bed by Schuyler Jackson, whom she would marry later, Graves "still regarded Laura as a kind of deity. . . . He still wanted to work, knowing that everything he wrote could be submitted to the critical scrutiny of her brilliant mind." Certainly these were not ordinary people, these private lives not those of the social comedies Noel Coward wrote.

This is Robert Graves's biography but Laura Riding's book—she commands it as she did her inner circle. The deference her admirers paid was a tribute to pure mind. Her origins could hardly have been more humble: her parents were poor Jews named Reichenthal who emigrated from Germany to New York. Her father was a tailor; the family did not prosper; they changed addresses frequently and Laura attended a dozen schools. At Girls' High School in Brooklyn she distinguished herself, winning scholarships that took her to Cornell University. There she married a fellow student, Louis Gottschalk. The marriage was not proving happy; she threw herself into writing fiction and poetry and adopted the name Riding as more suitable for a poet than Gottschalk.

She published poems in *The Fugitive,* a magazine in Nashville to which John Crowe Ransom, Allen Tate, and Donald Davidson also contributed. They found her formidable, a woman of definite and strong opinions. She had an affair with Tate, then divorced Gottschalk and moved to New York, where she became one of a literary crowd, being seen at parties with Hart Crane. At the end of 1925 she traveled to Europe to collaborate with Graves on a book about modern poetry. Collaborating with him was followed by cohabiting and taking charge of his life and work. They lived together in Majorca, where they supported themselves by writing and they dabbled in real estate, until during the Spanish Civil war they were compelled to leave for England.

What was the nature of the power Laura Riding exerted? Graves spoke in a poem of her ability to make "strange things" happen by the "strong pulling of her bladed mind." The biographer remarks that "when Laura Riding was exerting the full force of her personality, it had often seemed to those around her that she was possessed of paranormal powers." Some who disliked her said she was deranged; others called her a witch.

Robert's half-brother Richard, a senior member of the Egyptian civil service, had a simpler explanation: she was a "racial disease," meaning she was a Jew. Richard was very angry: Robert had given up a professorship at Cairo University, breaking his contract, and this would not do Richard's career any good. The couple's "new scale of values" frequently gave Robert's middle-class family cause for alarm; they had much to put up with and, with one or two exceptions, they tried to understand and forgive. One comes away from Richard Graves's book with a sense of strong family affection, not the least that displayed by the biographer. It could not have been easy to write about Laura Riding with a calm mind. The best description I know of the kind of power she possessed is by Salvador Dali, who claimed to have the same effect on people, an ability to bend them to his will and make them act out his ideas. He called it "paranoaic delirium . . . an active element determined to orient reality . . . an assertive, conquering force."

This is not a critical biography; it offers hardly any literary criticism, no examination in detail of works or the style in which they are written. For this kind of understanding we must go to the works themselves and the essays Robert Graves and Laura Riding wrote. As his books are in every library and hers are hard to find, I shall confine my remarks to the latter. Laura Riding could be a biting critic—see her essay "The Case of Monsieur Poe." It is hard to believe anyone could ever again take Poe seriously after this exposure of his bad taste and cheap effects. But in the same book, *Contemporaries and Snobs,* she pays considerable attention, almost respect, to Edith Sitwell, who was made out of the same papier-mâché as Poe. Laura Riding's reactions to literature were entirely personal, like her reactions to people. This accounts for the intuitive brilliance of her criticism and also for her lapses.

What of her poetry? It had an influence at the time, not to be measured by copies sold but by its effect on other poets. She and Graves believed that poets wrote for other poets. "True poets," Graves said, "will agree that poetry is spiritual illumination delivered by a poet to his equals, not an ingenious technique of swaying a popular audience or of enlivening a sottish dinner party." Her poems had an effect on the young Auden—he paid her the compliment of copying her style: economy of syntax, sparseness of sensuous detail, powerful rhythms. Here are three lines by Laura Riding:

> The standing-stillness
> The from foot-to-foot
> Is no real illness

and three by W. H. Auden:

> This gracious greeting
> "Good day. Good luck."
> Is no real meeting.

Today Laura Riding is almost forgotten. *The Norton Anthology of Modern Poetry,* that weathervane of poetic fashion, does not include her. The poetry, indeed, is not attractive. It is written in the language of her inmost thought, created out of her life and the lives of those moving in her orbit, out of research in mythology and some knowledge of psychology. The poems seem to have been written with difficulty, against a wish to be silent and self-contained. They, like her life, suggest more than they say; they are very different from any other kind of poetry we have in the United States.

> Come, words, away to miracle
> More natural than written art.
> You are surely somewhat devils,
> But I know a way to soothe
> The whirl of you when speech blasphemes
> Against the silent half of language
> And, labouring the blab of mouths,
> You tempt prolixity to ruin.

The message is definitely not for the poetry-writing workshop, which is nothing if not prolix and doesn't depend on miracles.

Poetry and Word Processing

One or the Other, but Not Both

I wanted to learn something about word processors. *The Word Processing Book* by Peter A. McWilliams was recommended to me. It has all sorts of useful information: it tells students how, when they have bought a term paper, they may alter it with a word processor to suit their own "personal style." "If you're a drama major," Mr. McWilliams says, "and are forced to write a paper on medieval French tapestry to fulfill some obscure university requirement, then I can see that spending several days researching such a paper would be counterproductive and may interfere with one's education."

He has some encouraging words for poets as well as plagiarists. He asks: "Why are poets turning to computers in record numbers?" And he answers: "Personal computers, outfitted with a quality word processing program, allow a writer maximum freedom to rearrange, take from, add to, alter, correct—in a word, change—the material being written. Of all writers, poets do more rearranging, taking from, adding to, altering, correcting—in a word, changing—than anyone else. Hence, the benefits of word processing accrue quickly for poets." He demonstrates how Mother Goose rhymes could be "updated" with a word processor. I'll spare you the result—it's too god-awful.

These are the author's ideas, not the word processor's. But is the word processor just a tool? The gun lobby argues that guns are harmless in themselves—it depends on how they're

New York Times Book Review, January 3, 1988.

used. But guns suggest one way of settling an argument, and word processors induce us to function as they do. As Mr. McWilliams says, the word processor makes it easy to re-arrange, take from, add to. Words can be erased at the touch of a button and other words substituted. Blocks of words can be moved about without retyping the page. The reason for the word processor is change.

I once met a woman who told me she was writing a thesis about word processors. I said I wrote poems mostly and didn't think I needed one. "Poetry," she said, and nodded under-standingly, as you do when speaking to someone who has attacks of asthma when everyone else is welcoming the advent of spring. As I talked to her I discovered why I felt about word processors as I did. It wasn't because I couldn't learn to use one—almost anyone can use a word processor; I know a novelist who swears by his, and he cannot drive a car. And it's not because I write short poems and don't use many words. In writing a few lines of verse you can find yourself covering pages, writing a line over and over, changing a word.

But if I'm always rewriting, why object to a machine that makes rewriting easy? Because it makes rewriting easy. If I think I can easily change the next word and there's nothing final about what I'm writing, then the nature of my writing changes. Poets don't think they're just writing—they think they are listening to a muse and that she doesn't stammer. A pressure to say a thing in a certain way and no other drives the poem forward from phrase to phrase and line to line. The idea of perfection—call it an illusion if you will, but a neces-sary illusion—drives the poem from beginning to end. If po-ets thought the words could be changed, the rhythm adjusted later, or that they could negotiate endlessly with the muse, they would destroy the sense of urgency that is the very life of the poem.

I can see where a writer of prose might find a word proces-sor a useful, perhaps indispensable tool. Not all writers of prose—some are poets, though not in verse. Their sentences are concentrated, vivid, and rhythmically apt. I do not think Flaubert would have written prose more easily if he had owned a word processor—he complained that sometimes it took him a whole day to write a sentence. If the author of *The Word Processing Book* had urged Hemingway to use a word processor for "the creation of new and remarkable forms of human expression for the illumination of us all," I think Hemingway would have told him to go to hell.

But many writers of prose could use a word processor. I recall a novel by Norman Mailer that consisted largely of taped conversations. It surely doesn't matter which words come next if you're reading Jacqueline Susann or Sidney Sheldon—it's the content that counts. I imagine anything that makes the mechanics of such writing easy would be a useful tool—anything, in Mr. McWilliams's phrase, that would "just free the mind."

But poetry isn't free. It works according to rules. Rules of meter obviously, and the rhythm of free verse is the most exacting of all, for it has to be perceived at every moment. You can't write free verse by counting the beat on your fingers. As you write, every word has to convey the rhythm you want, and no other word will do. The word has to be fixed on the instant. Finding the right word cannot be put off for a later time, for the rhythm of the words that will follow depends on the rhythm of this one. If the next word isn't right, everything that follows will be off.

Rhythm isn't the only thing that has to seem perfect. You must feel that every word has the exact shade of meaning you want, for that will affect the tone of what follows. I wrote a poem about working in a publishing house. It begins: "Even after J. B. left and went to a better house / I still sat there reading manuscripts. . . ." If I had said: "Even after J. B. died and went to a better house," the tone would be quite different. The second version is more amusing, and some may prefer it, but I didn't want to be satiric. I wanted the poem to seem true.

As I have said, poets do have to make changes, but they cannot think so; they must think that the next word and phrase will be perfect. At times, and these are the happiest, they have the feeling that words are being given to them with absolute finality. The word processor works directly against this feeling; it tells you your writing is not final. And it enables you to think you are writing when you are not, when you are only making notes or the outline of a poem you may write at a later time. But then you will feel no need to write it.

Poets, indeed, are a strange race, "wrecked," as one of them put it, "solitary, here." They don't think like the majority. Sometimes efforts are made to redeem them and bring them into the fold. Some years ago C. P. Snow spoke of "two cultures" and deplored the ignorance of science among people who were otherwise educated. He called for universities to make courses in science obligatory. I wondered what universities he had in mind, for the one I went to had indeed required attendance in such courses, and I found myself, as a last resort, taking a course in astronomy. One night a week, with others who were in the same fix, I went to an observatory on Morningside Heights and peered through a telescope at the cloud of dust and chemicals one kind of culture produces. As the sky could not be seen, we pointed the telescope at Times Square and read marquees advertising "Let Freedom Sing" and "Star and Garter" (featuring Gypsy Rose Lee). We studied the face that smoked a Camel and puffed smoke rings.

For two hundred years, ever since the French erected a monument to reason and danced around it, science has been the prevailing faith. And now science's child, technology, appears to be on the verge of a total triumph. I think, however, there is a resistance. I find it in myself—it seems to have been born with me—and I think there is a minority that feels as I do. We feel a truth in us that is difficult to express, for it involves our whole being. This truth has one thing to say at a time and only one way of saying it—an absolute language and form. Our task is to listen to it. Poetry isn't writing, not really. It is the art of listening.

This way of thinking is opposed to that which deals with ideas, ideas received in the marketplace, processed and carried to market and sold again. For that kind of commerce the word processor is ideally suited. We can always change our ideas. There's no truth in us, only an idea that serves the occasion. We ourselves are merely an extension of the machine, the part that puts in ideas.

I won't be using a word processor tomorrow, or a hundred years from now. I'll still be listening for the voice of the absolute. Edmund Wilson, a writer of prose, said verse was a dying technique. But in fact, it is not a technique, and we who write it are not dying as long as we believe in a reality that speaks in no uncertain terms.

First Books

Robert McDowell's long poem, "Quiet Money," is the story of a bootlegger, Joe, who flies the Atlantic and back when Lindbergh is flying it one way. Joe can't tell about his achievement because he was transporting gin, so Lindbergh cops all the glory and Joe remains unknown. But, as Joe says, "Headlines cut the pants off privacy," and some years later this is proved by the kidnapping of the Lindbergh baby. Joe pilots the police around as they follow up false leads. In the wake of this tragedy he concludes: "Son, you have to lose to win / . . . You know what it meant to me? / My daughter safe, first of all."

It's not just the good story, a rarity in poetry, that makes "Quiet Money" important: we can believe that the character would think in these words. This writing goes a long way to restoring the credibility of narrative in verse. If it is to be restored it must deal with events such as this—not epic journeys across the plains, but modern scenes with language such as people use. As he flies toward home Joe sees Lindbergh's plane below him, going the other way:

> a silvery image before him, skimming the sea.
> *Bird*, then *dolphin* occur to him. Then *plane*.
> That can't be, so he tells himself *reflection* . . .
> The image below him fades, heading the other way.
> That's wrong.

Review of Robert McDowell's *Quiet Money* and Thomas Lynch's *Skating with Heather Grace* in *Washington Post Book World*, May 3, 1987.

The language draws depths of meaning from the story: Joe's life is not reflected by Lindbergh's, and Lindbergh's will go wrong. In all strong writing the language comes out of the subject. Academic criticism prefers it the other way: words that relate to other words, and criticism to tell us what they mean. I think that *Quiet Money*, McDowell's first collection of poems, signals a change: poetry is leaving the academy. . . .[1]

The jacket of Thomas Lynch's *Skating with Heather Grace* says that he's an undertaker, and there's some talk of the profession in his poems. I never knew it could be so entertaining. His style is sinewy, full of surprise, and the rhythms make you think again. He has a funnily abusive poem, "For the Ex-Wife on the Occasion of Her Birthday," which lists all the bad luck he will not wish on her:

> Let me say outright that I bear you no
> unusual malice anymore. Nor
> do I wish for you tumors or loose stools,
> blood in your urine, oozings from any orifice.
> The list is endless of those ills I do not pray befall you.

There is a name for this rhetorical device—Lynch gives the impression of being well educated, not a bad thing in a poet . . . it keeps references to art, literature, and so on out of the poems.

Though Lynch writes about death and other losses he is never lugubrious, for he clearly takes such pleasure in the writing. The poem, "A Good Death Even When It Kills You," for example . . . A man, knowing he is going to die, goes out in a snowfall to fish. His wife goes out to find him and

> When she could see no farther, she began to hate him
> for fifteen years of rearing children and
> for cold nights when she warmed against him and for

---

1. This was wishful thinking. Poetry has not left the academy—many American poets earn a living by teaching in a university, and this affects their writing in all sorts of ways. See Dana Gioia on this, in my article, "On the Neglect of Poetry in the United States," reprinted in this volume.

all the tender habits he observed in love, because
he was all she'd ever wanted and was dead at forty,
spudding the ice for a hole, to get a line in.

Lynch knows how to write and end a poem. There are no false notes in this, his first book. It comes, I am glad to say, without a single jacket blurb.

An Obsessed and
Original Imagination

Robert Hass's introduction to *Rock and Hawk: A Selection of Shorter Poems by Robinson Jeffers* is a model of what introductions can be: informative, perceptive, and well written.

> If [Jeffers] did not have a vision, he had a series of insights that came to have the quality of a vision. There is first of all a sense of terrible and tormenting violence at the center of life, from the hawk's claw to the fury of war to the slow decay of stone. And there was also a sense, sharply, of something pained, divided and deeply sick in the human heart, at the root of sexual desire and religious longing. And finally there was the leap— to the wholeness of things, a leap out of the human and its pained and diseased desiring into the permanence and superb indifference of nature. The possibility of this leap became at first the central wish and, finally, the doctrine of his poetry.

Hass explains why Jeffers continues to be read, however peculiar and obnoxious his ideas may be: "Everywhere, and usually when one feels least comfortable, one feels the presence of a truly obsessed and original imagination."

The coast at Carmel provided Jeffers with hawks, vultures, and other creatures of the wild, and some splendid scenery. He appears to have had little interest in the matters that concern men and women every day. "Civilization," he tells us in "New Mexican Mountain," "is a transient sickness," and in "Gray Weather" he anticipates the extinction of the race with

Gettysburg Review, Winter 1988.

a certain satisfaction, a time when "life has no more desires than a stone":

> in the timeless quietness,
> One explores deeper than the nerves or heart of nature, the
>   womb or soul,
> To the bone, the careless white bone, the excellence.

A resentment like Ezra Pound's at being pushed aside by "the march of events" made Jeffers say some bitter things about America during World War II: in his view we were no better than the Nazis we were fighting. "There is something to be said for the bitterness and bluntness of the poems of this period," says Robert Hass. I would like to know what it is—to most readers Jeffers's opinions will seem unintelligent. There is a good deal of blather in Jeffers that has to be set aside if one wishes to pay attention to the writing.

I was recently reminded of Robinson Jeffers in dramatic fashion. I was in my study, which doesn't face the ocean—a depressing thing to contemplate steadily . . . no wonder the ocean-obsessed Jeffers had such little hope for humankind—when there was a terrific thump on the window. I went outside and saw a large gray thing sitting on the ground. A hawk, my God! I could see myself trying to pick it up and take it to the vet. The beak was everything that, in Jeffers's poems, a hawk's beak is said to be. At the moment Willa, Custis, and Veronica were down by the fence barking at some children who pass that way every day, and would soon be here to receive my thanks for a job well done. But then the hawk gathered its strength and, head tilted to one side, launched itself in the air and went staggering through the trees, like W. C. Fields at a studio party. I thought what a poem Jeffers might have made of it; as we see in "Hurt Hawks," he had the grand style, and pity . . . for wild things.

> I'd sooner, except the penalties, kill a man than a hawk; but
>   the great redtail
> Had nothing left but unable misery
> From the bone too shattered for mending, the wing that
>   trailed under his talons when he moved.

We had fed him six weeks, I gave him freedom,
He wandered over the foreland hill and returned in the eve-
    ning, asking for death,
Not like a beggar, still eyed with the old
Implacable arrogance. I gave him the lead gift in the twilight.
    What fell was relaxed,
Owl-downy, soft feminine feathers; but what
Soared: the fierce rush: the night-herons by the flooded river
    cried fear at its rising
Before it was quite unsheathed from reality.

Grandeur has gone out of our view of things. Other quali-
ties have taken their place—humor for one. But the note we
hear in the *Old Testament?* In Milton and *Lear?* Jeffers had it in
him, and when he was touched, and wasn't pontificating, he
could write poetry of a kind, towering—the word suggests
itself—that we have not had in America since.

This new collection of Jeffers's shorter poems shows what
he could do . . . and what he might have done, had he not
been wedded to hawks and stones. This, for example, from
"October Week-End," that I had not seen before:

It is autumn still, but at three in the morning
All the magnificent wonders of midwinter midnight, blue
    dog-star,
Orion, red Aldebaran, the ermine-fur Pleiades,
Parading above the gable of the house. Their music is their
    shining,
And the house beats like a heart with dance-music
Because our boys have grown to the age when girls are their
    music.
There is wind in the trees, and the gray ocean's
Music on the rock. I am warming my blood with starlight, not
    with girls' eyes,
But really the night is quite mad with music.

On the Neglect of Poetry in the
United States

There has been considerable talk about poetry in the United States, not because people are reading it but because they aren't. In an article in *Commentary* in August 1988, Joseph Epstein said that the neglect of poetry was the fault of the poets; they don't write as well as the modernist poets of the early decades of the century. Many American poets teach in universities and this makes their writing academic and obscure . . . it has nothing to say to the common reader. A year later the poet Donald Hall published a rebuttal in *Harper's*: he cited the large sales figures of some poets' books, and he said there were many poetry readings. He seemed to think that American poetry was doing very well.

In May of this year, the poet Dana Gioia published an article in the *Atlantic* in which he commented on both Epstein's and Hall's opposing points of view. Yes, many books of verse are published in the States every year, and many poetry readings are taking place, mostly on college campuses. On the other hand, the books are read by no one but poets and would-be poets, and the audiences at readings are composed of the same people, those who have a professional interest in poetry, that is, poetry as a means to getting a job . . . teaching "creative writing." Gioia blames the proliferation of university writing programs for creating a "subculture" of poets in universities who teach poetry-writing workshops, publish one another's writing in magazines and anthologies, and praise one

New Criterion, September 1991.

another's writing in reviews. No honest criticism of contemporary verse is being published, and the public has grown skeptical of poetry altogether. It was different forty years ago when a fearless critic such as Randall Jarrell was writing. Jarrell didn't hesitate to poke fun at the anthologist Oscar Williams though he knew this would keep him out of Williams's anthologies. An anthology of American verse these days is filled with the mediocre poems of creative-writing teachers, and, says Gioia,

> The proliferation of literary journals and presses over the past thirty years has been a response less to an increased appetite for poetry among the public than to the desperate need of writing teachers for professional validation. Like subsidized farming that grows food no one wants, a poetry industry has been created to serve the interests of the producers and not the consumers.

Gioia has some suggestions for remedying the situation. When poets give poetry readings they should read the works of other poets as well as their own, the way Dylan Thomas used to do. Poets should give readings together with performances of music. Poets should write prose about poetry more often and more candidly. "Anthologies," Gioia says, "are poetry's gateway to the general culture. They should not be used as pork barrels for the creative-writing trade." Anthologies should be made up of masterpieces that move and delight the reader. Poetry should be performed more and analyzed less: "Poetry needs to be liberated from literary criticism. Poems should be memorized, recited, and performed." In line with this, "poets and arts administrators should use radio to expand the art's audience. . . . Mixing poetry with music on classical and jazz stations could re-establish a direct relationship between poetry and the general audience."

These are practical suggestions—it is possible that these measures might make a difference, winning back a few thousand intelligent readers who think that poetry is not for them. Anything that can take the writing and reading of poems out of the university and directly to the public is all to the good. I agree that the teaching of creative writing in universities has done a great deal of harm. On the one hand, it produces quantities of mediocre verse such as fill the pages of the *American Poetry Review.* At the same time, as Gioia says, "Seeing so much mediocre verse not only published but praised, slogging through so many dull anthologies and small magazines, most readers—even sophisticated ones like Joseph Epstein—now assume that no significant new poetry is being written. This public skepticism represents the final isolation of verse as an art form in contemporary society."

My own experience in teaching writing courses backs up Gioia's remarks about the "subculture." I admit to having taught such courses—not often, but often enough to have formed a definite opinion of them. Universities offer courses and degrees in creative writing because they are profitable . . . to the university. Many people would like to be writers and will pay good money to be told that they are. A teacher of creative writing is expected to encourage students—a very different thing from giving honest criticism. "But," says the administrator, "we're very strict in admitting students. The ten students in your section are among the very best students we have." This may be so, but of ten such students perhaps two have the slightest chance of developing into poets. So you are giving the others a false hope. But the administrator is not at a loss—he has another line of defense to fall back on. "Even if the others never write a poem for the rest of their lives, they will have gained invaluable experience: they will have learned what it is like to create, from the inside." A nice line of argument, but entirely hypocritical: this is not the way such courses, workshops in writing poetry and fiction, are presented to the students. They enter them thinking that, by being exposed to the comments of a writing-teacher, and their fellow students, they will be made into writers.

If I think of the poets of my generation, or those who came before us, not one of them was made a poet by taking courses in creative writing. They learned by reading, writing, and knowing one or two people who would criticize what they wrote. A remark by Edward Gibbon should be placed above the entrance to every writing program in the United States: "The power of instruction is seldom of much efficacy, except in those happy dispositions where it is almost superfluous."

The students I had in a poetry-writing workshop were amazingly ignorant. They wanted to write poetry because they were far more interested in their own feelings than in the feelings of other people . . . they knew hardly anything of history, philosophy, or religion. What they did know about was writing as a career—the names of successful poets were often on their lips, the ones who were awarded prizes and who frequently gave poetry readings. The writing students were blown about by every wave of fashion . . . "Have you written your Jorie Graham poem yet?" While they were criticizing one another's poems they were learning nothing. One thing they weren't learning was the forms of verse that had developed over the centuries. They didn't know anything about meter, so they could only write free verse. This was usually a monologue, prose that went galumphing, the lines breaking where they shouldn't and stumbling in and out of meter.

So I agree with Gioia's description of the "subculture"—it has produced much bad writing and driven the public away from verse. Where I part company with Gioia—and with Joseph Epstein and Donald Hall—is in their emphasis on the public function of poetry. Is that really the main concern? When I think about poets of the past whose works I love: Dante, Chaucer, Milton, Wordsworth, Whitman . . . or the great poets of this century: Yeats, Rilke, Akhmatova, Eliot, Jiménez, and a dozen others . . . was their relationship to the public a main concern? They thought about the public, of course . . . how could they avoid it? If they lived in exile, as did Dante and Jiménez, they were grieved at being separated from the life they knew. If they were at odds with their countrymen, as were Milton and Wordsworth, they felt just as isolated as those who lived in exile. Yeats was a senator, but as a poet he felt isolated, fearful of growing old and being out of touch with younger minds. But these were secondary considerations: for these poets, their relationship to the public was not the first thing on their minds. Other matters were more important: politics, philosophy, religion . . . but, above all, the act of writing. Their main concern was wresting poetry out of the seemingly incoherent stream of experience. I am not saying that they did not want to be published and heard . . . obviously they did. But this was only an afterthought.

This is why I part company with those who write about bringing poetry to the public, acute as their observations may be. I think they place the emphasis entirely on the wrong thing. It doesn't matter in the least if a poet sells thirty thousand copies of a book or a hundred copies. All that matters is what is in the book and how well it is written. I could list names of poets who in their day sold their tens of thousands and whose writing today doesn't matter to anyone at all. Does anyone today read Bailey's *Festus?* Yet in the nineteenth century Bailey was held by many to be a better poet than Tennyson or Browning. The relationship of the poetry to the public is a matter for historians of culture to ponder—it is of no real concern to the poet or to lovers of poetry.

The poets I have named—Dante, Chaucer, and the rest—were great poets. To talk of greatness makes some people uneasy. They don't like talking on such a high plane. Sophisticated people are afraid of seeming naïve . . . maybe they have a memory of childhood they wish to suppress . . . a tyrannical parent or teacher. They aren't at all prudish about sex but they are embarrassed by any mention of spiritual life. If you use the word "great" you are likely to be called idealistic or romantic. In university departments of the humanities greatness is not mentioned—academics prefer a sociological view of the human mind and its productions, for people can be trained to think as a group, whereas greatness has no need of teachers. The poststructural theorists who for the past twenty years have infested American universities have given a philosophical underpinning to the distrust of greatness: deconstructionists don't believe in authors, much less in calling any writing great. According to the followers of Derrida and de Man, poems aren't written by individuals, they are written by the language we use, that is, by society. You have heard the theories, I am sure, and I don't mean to waste my time on them—they will soon return to the dark. But, as I have said, many readers feel uneasy about locating the impression they receive from a work of art in some quality of the artist's mind. Yet it is the most obvious thing in the world that for art to be great, for it to reach out to people, to move and delight them, it must proceed from a man or woman who is great.

Dana Gioia's suggestions for bringing poetry to the public sound plausible, but they attack the problem from the outside, suggesting certain practical measures that could be taken. In this his approach is typically American. But he doesn't speak of the one thing, the only thing, that can surely make a difference. He doesn't speak of the demand that poetry be great. This is what the public wants . . . anything less is not going to please it. Performances of mediocre poems will not make the public like poetry any better. It has always been possible to fill an auditorium for an evening of poetry by a visiting Russian poet, or a group of poets protesting something or other. But these occasions have not made the public like poetry the day after. Only a great poem, a poem it remembers, can make it do that.

Poetry is writing, not performance. Some people disagree— they think poetry should be performed. But if poetry is one of the performing arts it must compete with television, theater, and movies. There is a very clear danger to the poet who believes in performance: he will stress theatrical elements at the expense of thought. There is a communion between writer and reader that cannot take place when poetry is read aloud to a roomful of people.

Can poetry compete with rap lyrics? The songs of Bob Marley? The squirming of Madonna? I wrote to Gioia saying that poetry could not compete with television, and he replied that the potential audience for poetry he had in mind was not TV viewers but 2 percent of the population. But this is not an answer to my basic objection: he was urging the poet to be a performer. Every step you take in that direction is a step away from poetry. The work of the poet is writing. All other efforts detract from this.

"No art," a poet said, "ever grew by looking into the eyes of the public." Amen to that. But then you have to think that poetry is an art, and that the poet aims to make it grow. If you conceive of poetry as entertainment, which is what reaching out for a wider audience requires, then by all means do everything you can to increase your audience. But will it be an audience for poetry or for theatrics—an attractive personality, a striking emotional delivery? The people who would rather have their poetry in performance are not lovers of poetry but of performance.

I don't believe in poets' trying to reach the public . . . poetry is bound to lose that battle. I believe with Keats that the world is a vale of soul-making, and I believe that it is the poet's task to help us make our souls by showing us how he makes his. An American novelist put it well. "Art," said Flannery O'Connor, "is not anything that goes on 'amongst' people. . . . It is something that one experiences alone for the purpose of realizing in a fresh way, through the senses, the mystery of existence."

The way to overcome the present neglect of poetry is to write great poems. If poets can do this they don't have to worry about being neglected. If not tomorrow, or ten years from now, one day their poems will be read and appreciated. I believe this with all my heart. If I did not believe this I would have stopped writing long ago. Every time I sit down to write, it is in the hope that I shall write well . . . better than I have written before. At such times the public is the furthest thing from my mind.

> Fame is the spur that the clear spirit doth raise
> (That last infirmity of noble mind)
> To scorn delights, and live laborious days;
> But the fair guerdon when we hope to find,
> And think to burst out into sudden blaze,
> Comes the blind Fury with the abhorred shears,
> And slits the thin-spun life. "But not the praise,"

Phoebus replied, and touched my trembling ears;
"Fame is no plant that grows on mortal soil,
Nor in the glistering foil
Set off to the world, nor in broad rumor lies,
But lives and spreads aloft by those pure eyes
And perfect witness of all-judging Jove;
As he pronounces lastly on each deed,
Of so much fame in Heaven expect thy meed."

If the word "Heaven" evokes resistance in the modern reader, the reader is at liberty to exchange it for some other, some acceptable word. In any case, Milton made the point I am trying to make. Poetry doesn't depend on "broad rumor." It comes from within the poet. If someone is listening, well and good. If no one is, so much the worse for the public.

And consider this: poems that were once thought obscure and out of the reach of all but a few initiates—the poems of the modernists whom Joseph Epstein says he admires, though I doubt he would have admired them at the time—are now in the anthologies. Chaucer, Dante, Wordsworth, and Whitman continue to find readers. How did this come about? Not because these poets had a mission to bring poetry to the public, but because, to borrow from Robert Frost, they were troubled by something in them. They had something to say and could say it well. I am sure that when Patrick Kavanagh wrote "The Great Hunger" he was thinking about life in Ireland, not about the public for his writing.

There are poets in the United States who, I suppose, could be said to be suffering from neglect. If they are suffering it is because they think they are. All that it takes to end the neglect of poetry is for the poets to stop feeling neglected and get on with their work. They need not be concerned about the matters Donald Hall is informed about: how many books of verse were sold and poetry readings given. They may ignore Joseph Epstein's low opinion of contemporary verse . . . what does this have to do with the poems they are writing? They may say to Dana Gioia, Thank you. The measures you advise might induce some people to attend performances of poetry and music, to listen to poetry on the radio, or even to read books of verse, but this is not what is uppermost in my mind. I am not thinking about the public, I am trying to accomplish what an American poet once said was the main task of the poet: to lift into poetry by an act of imagination things that are right under my nose.

This may seem a hard and lonely road. Well then, let us be lonely together. We owe it to the public to write as well as we can, and this requires solitary thought.

Strategies of Sex in
Whitman's Poetry

He wanted to be liked, to be thought of as a good companion, shirt open at the neck, hand on hip, a saunterer in the crowd. He would be "no stander above men and women or apart from them" (*LG* 52). Only Pharisees and hypocrites would find anything to murmur at in Walt Whitman's tolerance of an opium-eater or a common prostitute. If he stood up for the stupid and crazy, was this not the way laid down by the founder of Christianity?

But homosexuality was different. In the nineteenth century, deviant sexual behavior was regarded as a vice so abhorrent that it was scarcely ever mentioned, and certainly not in polite society. It was as though the reading public did not know what homosexuality was until, in 1895, Oscar Wilde brought his libel suit against Lord Queensberry, and "the Love that dare not speak its name" was made plain.[1] Whereupon there was a tremendous outcry, and Wilde was put on trial and sentenced to two years at hard labor.

Whitman was fully aware of the peril in which he stood; there were those who would severely condemn what he called love. In the poem titled "As if a Phantom Caress'd Me," the poet is walking with a lover. Here as elsewhere, the gender of

---

From a special issue of *Mickle Street Review* 11 (1989).

1. Lord Alfred Douglas used the phrase in a sonnet. Wilde explained it to the court as "a great affection of an elder for a younger man as there was between David and Jonathan." See Hyde, pp. 200, 201.

the lover is not specified, but the lover is the active partner, and I think there can be no question that the lover is a man.

> As if a phantom caress'd me,
> I thought I was not alone walking here by the shore;
> But the one I thought was with me as now I walk by the
>   shore, the one I loved that caress'd me,
> As I lean and look through the glimmering light, that one has
>   utterly disappear'd,
> And those appear that are hateful to me and mock me.
>
> (*LG* 447)

He was afraid of the hateful mockers. If he wished to write about love, he would have to do so in a manner that would be acceptable to the public. And he did want to write about love. He thought a great deal about love, especially the love of one man for another.

One way to make it acceptable would be to make it general—not the love of one man for another, but of men for one another. This would defuse the sexuality; no one objects to men being friends together. He would speak of a new kind of consciousness, a bonding between men.

> I will make the most splendid race the sun ever shone upon,
> I will make divine magnetic lands,
>   With the love of comrades,
>   With the life-long love of comrades. . . .
>
> I will make inseparable cities with their arms about each
>   other's necks,
>   By the love of comrades,
>   By the manly love of comrades.
>
> (*LG* 117)

And this love would be quite acceptable—indeed, for the good of the state. This poem, "For You O Democracy," concludes with the line: "For you these from me, O Democracy, to serve you ma femme!" The great female Democracy would be pleased to see men with their arms about each other's necks. Whitman frequently expresses this hope; the passage in "Song of Myself" which depicts the woman spying

on the young men bathing is a dramatic rendering of the
theme:

> Twenty-eight young men bathe by the shore,
> Twenty-eight young men and all so friendly;
> Twenty-eight years of womanly life and all so lonesome.
>
> (*LG* 38)

You know how it goes:

> An unseen hand also pass'd over their bodies,
> It descended tremblingly from their temples and ribs.

This, then, is what he will do: make the love of man for
man a general love—not the kind that lurks in corners, but
the kind that goes swimming and frolics in the open air.
Women will accept it, and the hateful mockers will be silenced.

But only if it is made to seem innocent . . . just holding
hands and putting their arms about each other's necks. Now,
whether Whitman himself had such platonic relations, or be-
lieved that they would come into being and be generally ac-
cepted, I have no way of knowing. I am concerned with his
poems, with how they are written and what they appear to say.
I think that many people have a mistaken idea of Whitman.
For example, they think he spoke frankly on the subject of
sex. I think they have swallowed his bait, hook, line, and
sinker.

Consider these lines from "Whoever You Are Holding Me
Now in Hand," one of the "Calamus" poems, in which, it is
said, Whitman reveals his homosexuality. He invites the
reader,

> first watching lest any person for
> miles around approach unawares, . . .
> Here to put your lips upon mine I permit you,
> With the comrade's long-dwelling kiss or the new husband's
> kiss,
> For I am the new husband and I am the comrade.
>
> (*LG* 116)

It may seem that he is declaring his homosexuality, for the kiss of the comrade is the same as a kiss between husband and wife. But let us suppose a reader who could hardly imagine that such a thing as homosexual love existed—that is, the common reader in Whitman's day. What then would be the effect of the passage? Rather than conveying the idea of sex between men, would the effect not be to make the comrade's kiss seem chaste? The idea of a male comrade behaving like a husband is too farfetched—it must be a figure of speech. One is accustomed to seeing such figures of speech in Scripture; is not Christ spoken of as a bridegroom? The "comrade's long-dwelling kiss," therefore, is a gesture of affection only, not desire.

At the same time, if the reader were homosexual he would see the kiss of the comrade for what it actually was—an expression of homosexual feelings. So Whitman could have his cake and eat it too—safeguard his reputation and express his hidden, illicit feelings to those who felt as he did.

The strategy worked, and he used it frequently. Gestures of love between men are made to seem just friendly. The confusion of love with friendship appears in "I Saw in Louisiana a Live-Oak Growing." The oak is "uttering joyous leaves all its life without a friend a lover near" (*LG* 127). "I am he," Whitman declares in "Song of Myself," "attesting sympathy." Sympathy is not sex. He is "extoller of amies and those who sleep in each other's arms" (*LG* 50). Who could find fault with such friendly relations? It is just affection and keeping warm.

In order to make the common reader think that "the dear love of comrades" is innocent—that is, asexual—Whitman defuses sex altogether. He makes the love of man and woman innocent, too. There is no erotic attraction. Yes, I know what he has to say in "I Sing the Body Electric," how painstakingly he describes sexual intercourse between a man and a woman. I shall return to this later; for the moment I shall say only that the description is unconvincing. In several places Whitman makes the woman a comrade like the male. She is not an object of desire, for all bodies, male and female, are the same, and the difference that creates desire has been eliminated. In "I Sing the Body Electric," he asks,

Have you ever loved the body of a woman?
Have you ever loved the body of a man?
Do you not see that these are exactly the same to all in all
    nations and times all over the earth?

(LG 99)

The audacity of this is breathtaking—not because it is frank,
but because it lies so bravely, telling the reader to disregard
what he knows, the evidence of the senses. In passages such as
this, Whitman is a very chaste poet—it would seem that, as
Paul urged, he has made himself a eunuch for Heaven's sake,
for his vision of a new consciousness, a nation of men openly
loving one another.

It is, however, a mask, and sometimes the mask slips. Then
we see that there is another side to the "love of comrades,"
one that is actively sexual. These lines from "Native Moments"
in the "Children of Adam" section of *Leaves of Grass* describe a
band of homosexuals on a bender:

Give me now libidinous joys only,
Give me the drench of my passions, give me life coarse and
    rank,
To-day I go consort with Nature's darlings, to-night too,
I am for those who believe in loose delights, I share the mid-
    night orgies of young men,
I dance with the dancers and drink with the drinkers,
The echoes ring with our indecent calls, I pick out some low
    person for my dearest friend. . . .

(LG 109)

Such admissions, however, are few and far between, and only
the occasional reader would know what Whitman was talking
about. To most readers, Whitman's keeping low company would
seem no more than that—disreputable, perhaps, but not a vice.

There is no sex about it—"brethren and lovers" are the
same. All bodies are the same: "The body of my love, the body
of the woman I love, the body of the man, the body of the
earth" ("Spontaneous Me," *LG* 104). When two are sleeping
side by side—"the one I love most lay sleeping by me under
the same cover in the cool night" ("When I Heard at the Close

of the Day," *LG* 123)—then who is sleeping by me? Man? Woman? It doesn't matter, for "Do you not see that these are exactly the same to all in all nations and times all over the earth?" ("I Sing the Body Electric," *LG* 99).

"It is a painful thing," he writes, "to love a man or woman to excess, and yet it satisfies, it is great" ("Starting from Paumanok," *LG* 21). But nowhere does he show the love of a particular man for a particular man, or of a man for a woman, or of a woman for a woman. Charley Shively finds the "Calamus" poems erotic (passim). But the loving comrade is not described and has nothing to say; one might be holding hands with a store-window dummy.

As I have said, and as D. H. Lawrence said long ago, love in Whitman is always general; it is never love for an individual. Love for the individual, that is, passionate love, is sometimes mentioned, but it does not have a face. Whitman's poetry speaks of love but does not enact it, does not show the drama of individuals loving and hating. There can be no drama, for there is no passion; and there is no passion because the element of sex that affects human behavior in all sorts of dramatic ways has been eliminated.

Another strategy was pretending to be a lover of women. I have mentioned the description of heterosexual intercourse in "Children of Adam":

> This is the female form,
> A divine nimbus exhales from it from head to foot,
> It attracts with fierce undeniable attraction. . . .
>
> ("I Sing the Body Electric," *LG* 96)

The description of intercourse follows. This must be one of the passages that offended reviewers of *Leaves of Grass*.

> Hair, bosom, hips, bend of legs, negligent falling hands all
>   diffused, mine too diffused,
> Ebb stung by the flow and flow stung by the ebb, love-flesh
>   swelling and deliciously aching.

It is, however, only a description—there is no passion in it, for, as I have said, there are no faces. The speaker might as well be describing gymnastics: "Without shame the man I like knows and avows the deliciousness of his sex, / Without shame the woman I like knows and avows hers" ("A Woman Waits for Me," *LG* 102).

All right, then, let us have sex without shame. But what about privacy? What about the wish of one particular individual to be with another particular individual? Without privacy there is no passion, and when Whitman describes heterosexual love, one has the impression that he got the positions right but the feelings wrong. As Lawrence says, "This poet with the private soul leaking out of him all the time. All his privacy leaking out in a sort of dribble, oozing into the universe" (*Studies* 178).

Woman in Whitman's poems is a receptacle and a vessel: "I pour the stuff to start sons and daughters fit for these States" ("A Woman Waits for Me," *LG* 102). She is part of the machinery of state, the part that has the liquid poured in and produces children. "I press with slow rude muscle, / I brace myself effectually, I listen to no entreaties" (*LG* 102). Poor woman! Obviously, having sex is no fun for her—it is positively painful. "I dare not withdraw till I deposit what has so long accumulated within me" (*LG* 103). This is, in fact, a description of rape. Yet there are those who think that Whitman was a pioneer, a liberator in matters of sex! I do not think that any woman reading these passages would think so.[2]

Of course, Whitman did not mean to be insensitive; the trouble came of pretending to be what he was not. And in his case, there was a pressure to show all sides of life—he was the poet of democracy. So he must also write about married love—but how clumsy and offensive this writing is!

Compare the lines I have been reading with these:

---

2. A reader of this essay points out that "many women, perhaps beginning with Anne Gilchrist, have regarded Whitman as a tender lover of women." I think that, being fond of Whitman, they saw in his poems what they wished to see. I doubt that a woman today who reads "A Woman Waits for Me" would think him a tender lover of women.

I mind how once we lay such a transparent summer morning,
How you settled your head athwart my hips and gently turn'd
over upon me,
And parted the shirt from my bosom-bone, and plunged your
tongue to my bare-stript heart,
And reach'd till you felt my beard, and reach'd till you held
my feet.

("Song of Myself," *LG* 33)

This is tender and authentic. It is private, as the description of heterosexual love was not—I feel that it is, for I feel that I am intruding. The speaker is not going at sex like a pile-driver—on the contrary, he seems to be the passive partner. We do not know the gender of his lover, but I am quite sure that this is a description of homosexual love. It is altogether superior—there is no talk here of the States, no bragging of his virility. He seems to be quite overwhelmed by the memory of the experience. It proves nothing—it simply is.

But the lines I have quoted are immediately followed by these:

Swiftly arose and spread around me the peace and knowledge
that pass all the argument of the earth,
And I know that the hand of God is the promise of my own,
And I know that the spirit of God is the brother of my own,
And that all the men ever born are also my brothers, and the
women my sisters and lovers.

(*LG* 33)

Did you think it was sexual intercourse? It was a mystical experience in which the soul merged with God and the whole human race.

So he defuses the sex, and *honi soit qui mal y pense.*

The movement from sex to God may have been quite natural. Whitman may have felt just as he says, and, apart from his own feelings, there was an ancient tradition of mixing sex with God. Consider the Bible: "His left hand is under my head, and his right hand doth embrace me" (Song of Solomon 2:6). Consider the terms in which John Donne speaks to God:

Take me to you, imprison me, for I
Except you enthrall me, never shall be free,
Nor ever chaste, except you ravish me.

("The Holy Sonnets X")

In George Herbert's poem, Christ is a gentleman paying a call on his fiancée: "Love took my hand, and smiling did reply, / 'Who made the eyes but I?' " ("Love III"). We do not think habitually in figures of speech, as people did in other times. We are literal-minded and inclined to think that a mind that expresses religion in terms of sex is more concerned with sex than religion. But Whitman's reader, unless he were an initiate, would have read the passage as a description of a religious or mystical experience, no more.

The same is true of this passage:

As the hugging and loving bed-fellow sleeps at my side
    through the night, and withdraws at the peep of the day
    with stealthy tread,
Leaving me baskets cover'd with white towels swelling the
    house with their plenty.

("Song of Myself," *LG* 31)

The stealthy bedfellow who withdraws at dawn sounds like a male lover, but whoever the lover may be, the passage is immediately defused of its sexual implications. The "baskets cover'd with white towels" are a figure of speech such as one might find in the Bible. These baskets are from the Lord who provides "wine that maketh glad the heart of man, and oil to make his face to shine, and bread which strengtheneth man's heart" (Psalms 104).

Whitman's ways of writing about "the dear love of comrades" were effective; no one seemed to know what this dear love implied. Some early reviews of *Leaves of Grass* blamed the author for coarseness and indecency, but not the kind of indecency that, a generation later, would bring Wilde to picking oakum and working a treadmill. An unsigned review in the *Cosmopolite* of August 4, 1860, says that the book may be shocking, but "it is the poet's design, not to entice to the perversion of Nature, which is vice, but to lead us back to Nature, which in his theory is the only virtue" (Hindus 103). Another unsigned review, in the *Cincinnati Commercial,* 1860, described Whitman as "a person of coarse nature, and strong, rude passions," even "uncleanness," but nowhere was it suggested that he was recommending homosexual relations (Hindus 105–9).

In 1866, William Douglas O'Connor defended Whitman against the charge of indecency brought by James Harlan. Harlan had said that *Leaves of Grass* was "full of indecent passages" and that the poet was "a very bad man" and a "Free-Lover." "A better man in all respects," said O'Connor, "or one more irreproachable in his relation to the other sex, lives not upon this earth" (*The Good Gray Poet: A Vindication,* 1865; quoted in Hindus 119).

His "relation to the other sex"! What about his relation to his own? O'Connor could not have written in this way had not Whitman disguised his meaning.

But the disguise could be seen through. There were signals from Whitman to the reader who shared his feelings, just as there had been in the street. "O Manhattan, your frequent and swift flash of eyes offering me love" ("City of Orgies," *LG* 126). "Yet comes one a Manhattanese and ever at parting kisses me lightly on the lips with robust love" ("Behold this Swarthy Face," *LG* 126). And "an athlete is enamour'd of me, and I of him" ("Earth, My Likeness," *LG* 132).

How could such signals be missed by anyone? Very easily. Homosexuality was not a matter of general knowledge. As we have seen, not even book reviewers recognized it, and they were well informed.

There was, however, a sexual underground, men who knew one another at a glance. "I perceive one picking me out by secret and divine signs" ("Among the Multitude," *LG* 135). The good O'Connor missed the signals. He, along with the majority, was meant to miss them. But they would be seen by others. When Whitman says, "The sisters sleep lovingly side by side in their bed, / The men sleep lovingly side by side in theirs" ("The Sleepers," *LG* 425), there are two levels of meaning. One is for the common, heterosexual reader—the decent citizen who, if he knew what was really going on, could turn into a hateful mocker. This reader would hardly object to men who slept side by side like sisters. As a matter of fact, men did commonly sleep side by side, especially if they were poor. This custom lasted well into the present century. I do not recall, when I was a boy, anyone's suggesting that Laurel and Hardy were lovers. But among Whitman's readers, there were some who would have known what was intended.

I am not finding fault with Whitman for concealing his sexual preference. Consider the words of Mr. Justice Wills to Oscar Wilde: "that you, Wilde, have been the centre of a circle of extensive corruption of the most hideous kind among young men, it is . . . impossible to doubt" (Hyde 171). One cannot blame Whitman for protecting himself against this kind of humiliation and disgrace.

The character named Walt who appears in *Leaves of Grass* seems to speak his mind freely. But the author was not free, and at times he disguised his meaning, and at times played a part. Whitman was a great artist, and the misconceptions about him are a tribute to his art.

Works Cited

Hindus, Milton, ed. *Walt Whitman: The Critical Heritage*. London: Routledge, 1971.

Hyde, H. Montgomery. *The Trials of Oscar Wilde*. New York: Dover, 1973.

Lawrence, D. H. *Studies in Classic American Literature*. Garden City, N.Y.: Doubleday, 1953.

Shively, Charley. *Calamus Lovers: Walt Whitman's Working-Class Camerados*. San Francisco: Gay Sunshine Press, 1987.

Whitman, Walt. *Leaves of Grass: Comprehensive Reader's Edition*. Ed. Harold W. Blodgett and Sculley Bradley. New York: New York University Press, 1965. (Abbreviated as *LG*.)

"Planes in Relation"—the London Vortex

Wyndham Lewis says that the Vorticist group was "Art behaving as if it were Politics." He and a number of anti-Futurists—Epstein, Gaudier-Brzeska, T. E. Hulme, Wadsworth, and a "very muscular" cousin of Wadsworth's—went over to the Doré Gallery where Marinetti was lecturing and heckled the "Italian intruder."

Once Lewis and Marinetti found themselves together in a lavabo. Marinetti called Lewis a Futurist and Lewis denied it vehemently. He told Marinetti, "You insist too much on the Machine. You're always on about these driving belts, you are always exploding about internal combustion. We've had machines here in England for donkey's years. They're no novelty to *us*." Finally he said, "*Je hais le mouvement qui déplace les lignes.*"[1]

This was the theoretical basis of the Vorticists' opposition to the Futurists. (Another basis was envy—every new idea in art was being labeled Futurist). The Futurists were all for movement, the Vorticists wished to make geometric forms. In 1913 the Futurist Balla made a series of drawings of the vortex as an image of centripetal and centrifugal forces. A year later the vortex appeared in Wyndham Lewis's *Blast,* but not as Balla's dynamic image—forms of machinery had been con-

---

"Planes in Relation" was published in the catalogue of the International Conference on "Futurism and the Avant-Garde" held in Venice, Italy, September 26–28, 1986.

1. "I hate movement that displaces lines."

densed into a simple, abstract shape "spinning in space on an unshakeable axis."

Vorticist art was characterized by "sharpness and rigidity" (Gaudier-Brzeska) by "rigid reflections of stone and steel" (Wyndham Lewis). It was more difficult, however, to see how Vorticism could be applied to writing. Ezra Pound says that the Vorticists gave him a new sense of form. They made him "more conscious of the appearance of the sky where it juts down between houses, of the bright patterns of sunlight which the bath water throws up on the ceiling, of the great 'V's' of light that dart through the chinks over the curtain rings." All these were "new chords, new keys of design." He summed up his new sense of form in the phrase "planes in relation," and explained what this meant:

> The pine-tree in mist upon the far hill looks like a fragment of Japanese armor.
> The beauty of this pine-tree in the mist is not caused by its resemblance to the plates of the armor.
> The armor, if it be beautiful at all, is not beautiful *because* of its resemblance to the pine in the mist.
> In either case the beauty, in so far as it is beauty of form, is the result of "planes in relation."
> The tree and the armor are beautiful because their diverse planes overlie in a certain manner.

In the *Cantos* Pound will place one image next to another—like the pine tree and the armor—in an abrupt contrast that resembles the "sharpness and rigidity" of Vorticist painting and sculpture. In this way he reveals the form—that is, the "permanent idea"—they have in common. In the following passage an old story out of Provence is juxtaposed with a fragment of Greek mythology:

> Firm even fingers held to the firm pale stone;
> Swung for a moment,
>   and the wind out of Rhodez
> Caught in the full of her sleeve.
>   . . . the swallows crying:
> 'Tis. 'Tis. Ytis!

The woman is casting herself down from a height. As she does so the wind catches her sleeve and it looks like a wing. The crying swallows remind us of Procne who was changed into a swallow. These incidents, far removed in time, are juxtaposed in order to bring forth the form or "permanent idea" they have in common, metamorphosis, a unifying theme of the *Cantos.*

As early as 1912 Pound compared words to hollow cones of steel that radiated a force from their apexes. "The peculiar energy which fills the cones is the power of tradition, of centuries of race consciousness, of agreement, of association; and the control of it is the 'Technique of Content,' which nothing short of genius understands."

He applied the image of the vortex to the mind itself—the poet's mind was a vortex. "Emotion seizing upon some external scene or action carries it intact to the mind; and that vortex purges it of all save the essential or dominant or dramatic qualities and it emerges like the external original."

Images rush through the mind—"All experience rushes into the vortex. . . . It is every kind of whirlwind of force and emotion." But the mind itself, the vortex, does not change.

Pound's *Cantos,* a "poem containing history," let loose a torrent in modern poetry. After Pound it seemed that anything could come into a poem—history, mythology, personal reminiscences. But still there has to be a vortex, a mind to contain the flux and give it direction. Pound quotes Duhamel and Vildrac on the technique of poetry: *Mais, d'abord, il faut être un poète.*[2]

---

2. "But first you must be a poet."

James Wright

James Wright was born on December 13, 1927, in Martins Ferry, Ohio. His father worked for the Hazel-Glass factory across the river in Wheeling, West Virginia. In hard times he would be laid off, and then the family struggled with poverty and moved from one rented house to another. The poet has written about his father—if he wrote about his mother, this has escaped me. Perhaps his mother meant so much to him that he could not bring himself to speak of her, or perhaps she was not important to his writing. But only he could have given the answer.

Donald Hall has said that "Jim's whole life was compelled by his necessity to leave the blighted valley, to escape his father's fate."[1] The valley, the river, the factory appear repeatedly in Wright's poems, especially the early ones. So do an assortment of characters who are trapped by the environment or some pathological weakness and unable, as Jim did, to break free. He wrote as though, but for the grace of God, he would have been one of them, haunted by the specter of failure, a drunkard perhaps, or even a murderer. But though it may be tempting to read Wright's poems as keys to his life, he is not a confessional poet. His poems have been con-

---

This essay will also appear in a book on James Wright edited by William Roberson and published by Scarecrow Press.

1. Donald Hall, "Lament for a Maker," in *Above the River: The Complete Poems* (New York and Hanover, N. H.: Noonday Press and University Press of New England, 1990). Quotations of Wright's poems are from this volume.

structed to have a certain aesthetic and dramatic effect. They are works of the imagination.

Wright graduated from high school, served for two years in the army, and attended Kenyon College. John Crowe Ransom published two of Wright's poems in the *Kenyon Review,* one of the most prestigious magazines in the English-speaking world. In the 1950s and 1960s Wright published frequently and was much admired. He had come a long way from the Ohio valley and the losers who hung out in bars or drowned in the river. His private life was not happy. He had "nervous breakdowns," and a marriage ended in divorce. But he could feel sorrier for the characters he imagined than he was for himself. He was always thinking about poetry, the rhythm and sound of verse.

He began writing in meter, rhyme, and stanza . . . traditional forms. The poems in his first book, *The Green Wall,* are filled with old music—E. A. Robinson's cadences are particularly noticeable in the last stanza of Wright's "A Girl in a Window":

> Soon we must leave her scene to night,
> To stars, or the indiscriminate
> Pale accidents of lantern light,
> A watchman walking by too late.
> Let us return her now, my friends,
> Her love, her body to the grave
> Fancy of dreams where love depends.
> She gave, and did not know she gave.

In the late 1950s he would turn from meter and rhyme to free verse, but not as it is written in poetry-writing workshops, with a tin ear—Wright's has "the cadence of the musical phrase."

At this time he was translating foreign poets—in the *Complete Poems* a section of translations precedes the free-verse poems of *The Branch Will Not Break.* Wright's translation of Jiménez's "Moguer" is a far cry from the manner of E. A. Robinson:

> Moguer. Mother and brothers.
> The house, clean and warm.
> What sunlight there is, what rest
> In the whitening cemetery!

Robinson narrates and meditates in complete sentences, Jiménez wishes to communicate moments of heightened consciousness immediately with a few words. Feelings must be conveyed from the writer to the reader by evoking sense perceptions, and this means writing with images. There is plenty of imagery in Shakespeare, Donne, Milton, Keats, and Tennyson, but the poet who wishes to write lines that sound like speech, that is, free verse, having abandoned meter and rhyme must concentrate on images to convey his feelings. In the following passage Wright's feelings about the people of the Ohio valley are conveyed almost entirely through images:

> In the Shreve High football stadium,
> I think of Polacks nursing long beers in Tiltonsville,
> And gray faces of Negroes in the blast furnace at Benwood,
> And the ruptured night watchman of Wheeling Steel,
> Dreaming of heroes.

James Wright and Robert Bly are said to have started a school of Deep Image Poets. Critics like to put poets in school, but in fact there was no school, only a friendship of poets who were breaking with the forms and attitudes of traditional English verse and discovering new ways to write a poem. The ground had actually been prepared by Ezra Pound, T. S. Eliot, and William Carlos Williams around 1912 when they insisted on writing with images and the sound of speech, but the new poets, especially Bly, claimed they were illuminating parts of psyche not revealed before.

When Wright was transforming himself into the new kind of poet, with some regretful backward glances to meter and rhyme, he was a frequent visitor at the farm of Robert and Carol Bly. This lay in the southwest corner of Minnesota, flat land with fields of corn stretching to the horizon. It was hot in summer and the cicadas were singing. A storm might spring up with lightning and thunder. I went there a few times, and once Donald Hall and I came with our families. After breakfast the poets would separate to write . . . in the "chicken house" from which the chickens had been evicted or a room upstairs in the farmhouse. In the afternoon there would be walks or boating and fishing in a nearby lake. In the evening we would talk and read poems to each other, a poem we had just written or one we had discovered.

Robert and Carol were publishing their magazine, *The Sixties*, and thinking of ways to poke fun at writers they thought old-fashioned and reactionary or just plain stupid. Carol had a keen sense of social responsibility . . . she deplored the pollution of air and water by the military with their tests of the Atom Bomb. She was also the critic every writer would like to have, alert to every nuance—in years to come she would be an outstanding writer of prose. Our sessions were lively and often we disagreed. I had reservations about the poetry of Neruda, for example: his poems could be a parade of images and I found this tedious.

I did not think that one could reach out and appropriate the way of thinking of a poet in another culture. When an American tried to do this the result was strained and unconvincing. The following lines by James Wright, for example:

> Small antelopes
> Fall asleep in the ashes
> Of the moon . . .

To which I can only say, "Really?" It may be natural for a Jiménez to see antelopes sleeping in ashes on the moon, but it seems highly unlikely for an American. Some of the poetry Wright and Bly admired struck me as having no relation to the life around us.

It was another matter entirely when Wright wrote about something he had seen, in language that came naturally. In the following lines he is writing about a pony. The writing cannot be labeled surrealist or imagist . . . it appears not to be writing at all but the experience itself without, as Whitman said, "any elegance or effect or originality to hang in the way. . . . What I tell I tell for precisely what it is." The astonishing image with which the poem ends . . . this too seems natural. This is why it is so astonishing.

She is black and white,
Her mane falls white on her forehead,
And the light breeze moves me to caress her long ear
That is delicate as the skin over a girl's wrist.
Suddenly I realize
That if I stepped out of my body
I would break into blossom.

One evening at the farm Jim read aloud a poem he had writ-
ten about the Spanish poet Miguel Hernandez, who died in
one of Franco's prisons. When he had finished I said, "Why
are you so concerned about him when you're trying to kill
yourself?" Jim had been drinking whiskey all day and into the
night. He was also chain-smoking, and this would prove just
as lethal, though people didn't think so then.

My remark struck everyone dumb, and Robert took me
aside. He informed me that people born under the sign of the
Ram, as I was, were given to speaking bluntly. I think this was
his way of letting me know that I had hurt Jim's feelings.

No one else seemed to mind Jim's drinking, and when he
went on poetry-reading tours he was plentifully supplied with
liquor. Ever since Dylan Thomas visited the States there had
been a tradition of poets drinking themselves into a stupor. It
was expected . . . this was how a poet behaved. It was a sign of
genius.

Jim was under considerable pressure at the University of
Minnesota. He was coming up for tenure and there were
members of the faculty who did not take kindly to the idea of
having a poet for their colleague. Jim had a Ph.D. but in their
eyes as he was a writer he couldn't be a scholar. As Randall
Jarrell says, the critic tells the writer, "Go away, pig! What do
you know about bacon?" And if the pig has hangovers and
misses his classes . . .

At Jim's tenure hearing, the poet and critic Allen Tate
voted against him and he was fired. I suppose Tate did this in
order to protect himself and other writers in universities
against the charge that they were irresponsible. Whatever his
reason, Tate missed the opportunity to do a brave and honor-
able thing—he might have come to Jim's defense like the

chairman of the department of English in Seattle who for years protected Theodore Roethke. Today the scholars and critics of the University of Minnesota have been forgotten, but James Wright's poems are part of our heritage.

Hard times . . . but, as I have said, Jim was always thinking about poetry, and such a person is happy in ways most people cannot conceive. Besides, Jim was not a lugubrious man—he had a lively sense of humor. He did not write humorous poems—in the 1960s the only well-known poet who did was Allen Ginsberg. The others approached poetry solemnly as though it were a religion.

But Jim in person was good company. I ran into him once at an airport. We were giving poetry readings, Jim traveling in one direction, I in another. He had just been driven through the seedy part of town, passing by the strip joints. There was a theater with a marquee advertising . . . "Flesh Gordon"! Jim was still chuckling over it. "Flash Gordon," the space hero of the funnies . . . a New York accent . . . and voilà, a man wriggling his buttocks on the stage, "Flesh Gordon"! Now that I have told the story I can see that no one else may see the humor in it. I may think it funny because I remember how funny it seemed to Jim.

In 1966 Jim was hired by Hunter College in New York—he would live there for the rest of his life. A year later he and Edith Ann Runk, the Annie of the poems, were married, and in 1971 his *Collected Poems* was awarded a Pulitzer Prize—I was the chairman of the jury that awarded him the prize. But the real prize was Annie—she made him as happy as he could ever be.

But life and art do not always walk hand in hand. The poems that Jim was writing in the late 1960s and titled "New Poems" in both *Collected Poems* and *Above the River* are a falling off. The poet seems to think that he only has to tell us what he feels sincerely. There is an absence of color, imagery, compelling rhythm.

> I believe that love among us
> And those two animals
> Has its place in the

> Brilliance of the sun that is
> More gold than gold
> And in virtue.

In the late 1960s American poets were feeling more alienated then usual—the country was at war and the poets were against it. They protested, and some of them wrote poetry that was angry and bitter. Troubling yourself about finding the right words, the right image, saying a thing in a memorable way, seemed a frivolous occupation when people were being killed in Vietnam. When you wrote a poem you just wrote down what you felt. The result was often flat, prosaic, sentimental writing.

There is a recovery in the poems Wright published in *To a Blossoming Pear Tree* (1977) and the poems he wrote from then on. He and Annie traveled—the poems he wrote about Italy are as joyful as the poems about Ohio were grim. Once they stayed for a day at my mother's place at San Alessio, a few miles from Lucca. I have a snapshot of Jim floating in a rubber boat in the pool—he is a substantial, broad-chested man. At the lunch table he delivered himself of lines of verse . . . he thought that everyone in the world, perfect strangers, would care about a poem as much as he did. It was one of the lovable things about him . . . he was unique. I have never known anyone who loved poetry as much as Jim did.

His poems about nature are well known:

> . . . the bronze butterfly
> Asleep on the black trunk,
> Blowing like a leaf in green shadow.

But there is another kind of poetry he wrote that I think deserves to be equally celebrated, about the detritus of an industrial world. It is not only landscape, it is a human condition. The heart sinks on contemplating it . . . cinders, weeds, and brambles by a railroad track. One is never so alone as one can be in such places. The view remains printed on the mind . . . all life seems to have ended there:

When you get down to it,
It, which is the edge of town,
You find a slab of gritstone
Face down in the burned stubble, the stinkweed . . .

The place is not exclusively American—it is to be seen in England, Spain, Australia—it is the edge of town everywhere. Wright has described it more feelingly than any other poet I know. Others were only passing through . . . he had lived there in imagination ever since he was a child.

Jim died on March 25, 1980, of cancer. I saw him at Mount Sinai Hospital shortly before he died. Annie brought me to his bedside. He looked at me eagerly—there was something he wanted to tell me. But he could no longer speak. He seized his slate and scrawled some words but I could not make them out.

The quality that rises from Jim's poetry and his life is sympathy, generosity, sincerity . . . above all, a joy in life and writing. For him they were one and the same. Jim once said with irony that he would not be among the English poets when he died. That is true, he isn't, but he is among the American poets and we are lucky to have him.

Of Cows and Chaucer

New Poems by Les Murray, Mark Strand, and
Stuart Dischell

Les Murray writes about Australia in all its variety from farm
and bush to suburb. He likes to rhyme, which our poetry-
writing workshops wouldn't touch with a pole—it's untrendy.
But Murray doesn't seem to care what academics think:
"Love," he writes, "never gave up rhyme." Unfortunately, the
poem in which he defends rhyming has some poor examples,
as when he speaks of "high logics that make all seeming stabil-
ity / a void demeaned by scrutability?"

Whether he is rhyming or not, Murray has great powers of
imagination and no end of nerve. "The Cows on Killing Day,"
unrhymed, is a stunningly original poem: life seen from in-
side the herd's communal mind, "All me."

> All me have just been milked. Teats all tingling still
> from that dry toothless sucking by the chilly mouths
> that gasp loudly in in in, and never breathe out.

The herd has its good moments:

> big rolls of tight dry feed: lucerne, clovers, buttercup, grass,
> that's been bitten but never swallowed, yet is cud.
> She walks up over the tractor and down it comes, roll on roll

Review of Les Murray, *Dog Fox Field;* Mark Strand, *Dark Harbor: A
Poem;* Stuart Dischell, *Good Hope Road,* in *Boston Sunday Globe,* March
21, 1993.

and all me following, eating it, and dropping
   the good pats.

And its bad moment, suddenly and terribly, when the herd mind sees itself being slaughtered:

> A shining leaf, like off the bitter gum tree
> is with the human. It works in the neck of me
> and the terrible floods out, swamped and frothy. . . .

The author of the cow poem is also able to write about the political thinking of the mother of the Sultan of Turkey in the year 1812, as she considers whether to support the czar of Russia or Bonaparte in their coming war. You wouldn't think that such a subject could be engrossing, but Murray makes it so. He has a poem, "Spotted Native Cat," about a man who receives a check that bounces, and how he outwits the sender and, having done this, realizes that he's really on his opponent's side. At the moment of victory, when the debtor has been tricked into giving his creditor the amount needed to cover the bad check:

>   Rage
> slowly darkens the planed boards of his face:
> You've got it at the bank then?—
>   It's in a safe place—
>
> It almost rattled me, how instantly his gaze
> assumes the tranced blue of drought-time days,
> dismissing me.

Robert Frost couldn't have done better, and the use of rhyme in this poem is masterly. In form as well as subject, Les Murray is always doing something new. Writing *Dog Fox Field* must have been great fun.

Mark Strand's *Dark Habor: A Poem* is sure to maintain his reputation for graceful, thoughtful writing. The poem in forty-five parts is a sequence of meditations, ranging from elegiac to playful:

It is true, as someone has said, that in
A world without heaven all is farewell.
Whether you wave your hand or not,

It is farewell, and if no tears come to your eyes
It is still farewell, and if you pretend not to notice,
Hating what passes, it is still farewell.

This is Strand being playful:

The idea of our being large is inconceivable,
Even after lunch with Harry at Lutece, even after
Finishing *The Death of Virgil.* The image of a god,

A platonic person, who does not breathe or bleed,
But brings whole rooms, whole continents to light,
Like the sun, is not for us. . . .

If this is too elegant for your taste, you have missed the
irony. The people who prefer "a simple still life" and being
little, "An understanding that remains unfinished, unentire, /
Largely imperfect . . . ," will be ejected from their comfort-
able little world, perhaps into a place that is "light, / Like the
sun." All this the poet suggests with a few words at the end of
the poem: the world can be as small as we wish to make it, but
only "so long as it lasts."

Notes at the end of *Dark Harbor* identify poets and friends
alluded to in the poems: Jorie Graham, Wallace Stevens,
Rilke, Richard Howard, John Ashbery, Octavio Paz, Jules La-
forgue and, of all people, William Wordsworth. "What the
devil is he doing in that galley?" I asked myself. Wordsworth
said that he "wished to keep the Reader in the company of
flesh and blood," and to use the "very language of men." He
would have stared in wonder at the likes of Ashbery and
Graham, who do neither. In the poem in which he alludes to
Wordsworth, Strand says:

It's a pity that nature no longer means
The woods, nor the wilds, nor even our own
Worst behavior, . . .

I find it hard to believe that Strand cares about nature and the wilds. It is just a remark such as one makes among friends, to be amusing. These poems remind me of Auden's. He said that poetry was feigning, and in our time, especially in institutes and academies, Auden has things all his own way. "What is truth?" might be inscribed above the gate of every American university.

Another generation may have other manners. One possible direction is indicated by Stuart Dischell in his first book, *Good Hope Road*. The opening sequence, titled "Apartments," is like switching from channel to channel:

> She wishes she were older
> Or younger, wishes the sky were a little calmer,
> That it wouldn't rain on her driving errands,
> That she wasn't so late for her appointment,
> That the car's problem was really only the cables, . . .

The ideas and objects come at you pell-mell, but the streams of consciousness add up to form clear portraits. It is an interesting technique, one that I think he hit on after trying a little of this and a little of that. Some of the poems in the second part of the book, "Household Gods," read like workshop exercises:

> One summer I collected bottles,
> The whole backyard filled with them—
> Coke and White Rock and Hires and Ma's, . . .

And here is the workshop poem that has asthma instead of punctuation:

> a star fell in the sky
> Far away   in the yellow lights of a living room
> A woman was   closing out the night   leaning forward

But there are fine poems in this section, too, especially "Good Hope Road," about the way people and animals live in the United States, hopefully, without good cause.

There is a symbolic or allegorical quality in Dischell's descriptions. When the woman wishes "That the car's problem was really only the cables," more than a car is meant. But he doesn't intrude his own thoughts—"The natural object is always the adequate symbol." For all its seeming objectivity, and perhaps because of this, Dischell's writing enlists our sympathy. In the end poem of the "Apartments" sequence, the woman being described "plans to be a writer one day and live in the City of Paris." One wishes her luck with her plan to drink strong coffee at a round white table, to keep one flower in a blue vase, and to read the same twenty books as Chaucer.

Jamaican Poets

The publication of five Jamaican poets is timely following the award of a Nobel Prize to Derek Walcott, which has focused attention on Caribbean writing. The publishers, Peepal Tree Books, have done well by their authors: the editions are attractively designed and printed. There is excellent poetry to be found among the five, and some that only a sociologist could like. The bad writing, I am glad to say, is far outweighed by the good.

Earl McKenzie writes of a woman who has two different languages:

> Miss Ida speaks only English to God.
> Scholars cannot fault the diction
> of her graces and prayers . . .

But in her dealings with her fellow mortals:

> she speaks Creole,
> the tongue of the markets and the fields;
> the language of labrish,
> su-su, proverbs and stories,
> hot-words, tracings and preckeh;

In 1992 Peepal Tree Books (in Leeds, England) published the following books by Jamaican poets: Earl McKenzie, *Against Linearity;* John Figueroa, *The Chase: A Collection of Poems 1941–1989;* Velma Pollard, *Shame Trees Don't Grow Here . . . But Poincianas Bloom;* Rachel Manley, *A Light Left On;* Ralph Thompson, *The Denting of a Wave.* This essay appeared in *Caribbean Review of Books,* February 1993.

it is the way to get
hard-ears pickney to listen . . .

Miss Ida could be a schoolteacher. She isn't a poet—poets
have a mind and style of their own. Earl McKenzie writes in
conversational English. He is a Jamaican poet not because he
writes in the English of the King James version or Miss Ida's
"tongue of the market and the fields," but because he is a poet
and thinks of himself as Jamaican.

The writing in *Against Linearity* is clear and thoughtful,
quickening with anger when it speaks of violence and cruelty:

> mule hauling sustenance of man
> skin burnt with whip and sun
> tired hoofs slithering on parched asphalt
> foam rising endlessly in its tortured mouth
> eyes pained and wild
> eyes staring without comprehension

McKenzie writes free verse, as do all the poets under consider-
ation, though John Figueroa also includes some early poems
in meter and rhyme. McKenzie's "After the Hurricane, the
Moon" shows his most consistent mood, elegaic and quietly
evocative:

> After the hurricane, the moon
> poured its gold over the rubble.
>
> From our roofless house,
> now without TV,
> we watched it rising
> on the sky's screen. . . .

The poem concludes with an explanation of the poet's feelings:

> . . . we who watched
> from our shattered house
> felt both blasted and blessed.

How much better it would have been if McKenzie had spared
us the explanation and ended with these lines that come be-
fore it:

> The storm destroyed
> and the moon rose
> both going their way
> in nature's indifference.

This would have left us with something to think about. But when the writer tells you what he felt and thought he shuts you out of the experience. Not only McKenzie . . . all of these poets are liable to explain what their poetry means.

McKenzie has some poems of "social significance," and these are fairly predictable—a poem, for example, titled "The Lynching"—but "Burglar Bars" is original. This poem speaks of a topic, crime, that is discussed in every newspaper, but from a personal point of view. We are looking at the bars that are placed on doors and windows to keep crime out:

> Burglar bars have become an art form
> In this our nervous land.
>
> The masters of this renaissance of dread
> work in studios with apprentices:
> They work late at night
> Designing patterns of steel,
> Elegant geometries
> And shapes of plants and animals
> To keep the burglars out.

The poem ends:

> Only cold metallic webs of beauty
> Stand between us and the night.

This is not the kind of explaining I've been objecting to: the "cold metallic webs of beauty" present a new idea and leave the thinking up to us. There are other poems of this caliber in *Against Linearity:* Earl McKenzie is a poet with ideas and a fine control of language and the cadences of verse.

John Figueroa's *The Chase: A Collection of Poems 1941–1989* represents a lifetime of writing and is the bulkiest of the books published by Peepal Tree. The author has taught in universi-

ties and edited an anthology of Caribbean poetry. I was there-
fore surprised to come across these lines in his book:

> What is Barbados or Peru
> Provence or Rome
> But places which Any Man
> Can make their home?

I turned the pages hoping that this was an aberration, but I'm
sorry to say it wasn't: many passages would qualify for inclusion
in *The Stuffed Owl,* the classic anthology of bad verse. This for
example, from a poem titled "From the Caribbean with Love":

> . . . Why be proud
> of what
> You or I could not
> did not
> And would have done?
> We must know
> While not denying the nurture
> Of history and the permanent peace
> Of a lawn cared for for a thousand years
> We must know the span of now
> As many depend on the stretch
> Backward nearly forever.

This writing has no form and doesn't make sense.

With some difficulty I found a poem in *The Chase* that
could be read with pleasure, "The Garden, Green and Great."
This is from a description of the garden:

> Around the pond are sweet bowers
> Around the bowers green grasses
> Flecked with mauve and yellow blossoms;
> Red hibiscus, yellow
> Allamanda, purple bougainvillea
> Surround and dome the bowers.

This is followed by an equally attractive picture of four
women: "A delicate Chinese with almond eyes and yaourt
skin," "A tall black girl whose skin shines," a "white Juno," and

> . . . with a glitter and a tinkle glides
> The golden sari and black-bird blackness
> Of the Indian's hair.

So Mr. Figueroa is capable of writing well. The trouble, I think, is that he has not been required to do so. He has written for people who know very little poetry and are easily pleased.

In *Shame Trees Don't Grow Here . . . But Poincianas Bloom* Velma Pollard writes about history and her travels. The history is simple, like movies in the thirties about Drake and Hawkins and other English worthies—she has simply turned the values around so that these men were intruders in an idyllic world. As for Christopher Columbus,

> Perhaps they should have stoned him
> that first time he came
> or pelted poison from the arrow tips
> but too much gentleness
> third world of love
> offered to men who know not love
> and cannot comprehend it . . .

Her reference to a "third world" and use of the present tense brings her history up to the present: it's not just Columbus and the conquistadors she would like to meet with stones and poisoned arrows, but present-day intruders. It does not occur to her that her anger is the opposite of the peaceableness for which the Arawaks are admired.

It is the same when she travels out of Jamaica—she is filled with righteous indignation and sees only what she wishes to see. In upstate New York she finds:

> heads
> of head-hunters
> hunted by Harrimans.

The writer who could find this in Harriman, New York, could find a grievance anywhere. She prides herself on having "a shame Tree [that] exists in the conscience of most Jamaicans."

She might consider the tree that reminds you not to be so superior.

The poems in which she undertakes to instruct us are prosaic . . . lines without rhythm, language with no color. The poems subtitled "But Poincianas Bloom," which deal with experience and the world she knows at first hand, are livelier. Real history begins with observations such as these, in the poem "Bridgetown (summer '78)":

> Because the sea
> walks slowly in
> or lapping fast
> caresses every moment of your sound
> this city hands you heaven
>
> street side
> the city traffic rushes
> crowding the kitchen din
> crowding the gentle altercation
> child with child

The poems of Rachel Manley in *A Light Left On* are like Chopin preludes: a moment in a garden, a night with rain playing on the roof. There is regret for the Edenic, vanished world of a family. Sometimes she writes forcefully, as in the poem titled "Cropover":

> Now they have cut the canes
> and I don't know whether they leave
> like Jews hoarded off to Treblinka,
> or protesting children
> to Sunday school,
> but the land is gross and torn
> and I am afflicted.

At the beginning of this essay I said that it would not be a peculiar use of language that would identify a writer as Jamaican—a tourist could use it—but the writer's thinking of herself as Jamaican. Rachel Manley uses standard English, but I cannot imagine a more "Jamaican" poem than "Cropover." The essential thing, however, is that it is poetry of a high order. Questions of identity may be interesting but they are not essential.

The longest poem in *A Light Left On* is dedicated to the poet Rilke and evokes the volatile images and compaction of language in the *Duino Elegies*. Manley's brief lyrics can be enchanting, but "Raron" is on a higher level of achievement altogether: the poetry is not just personal, it moves into a larger world, the arena of myths and legends. The speaker is climbing one of the Alps and arrives at a graveyard. "Is it only the old who climb this mountain / pacing their weakened steps up the quiet path?"

> Pass through the gate, it neither opens
> nor shuts; only the body folds
> its curtains behind. Consider the rose
> who begins her journey closed.
> Come to the lawn of beds, each resting
> brave tucked into the sum of his worth.
> A host of crosses turns at the sound of steps
> their arms outstretched like mendicants
> beseeching memory for each one's
> mute constituent. They mark the place
> where man's imagination left its luggage
> as it journeyed on.

I look forward to the poems Rachel Manley may write as she gains confidence and moves, as in "Raron," beyond the lyric to express all that she knows and can imagine.

Ezra Pound said that we ask the poet to build us his world, and in *The Denting of a Wave* Ralph Thompson gives us places to walk around in and people and things to look at. He begins with a carpenter building a one-room house in Jamaica, in the bush, and ends with a Jamaican airman, who is stationed in Japan, looking at a fishing boat in Tokyo Bay and feeling homesick. Thompson's poetry is open to the world but always riveted to things as they are, wherever he may be. He is both a narrative and meditative poet, the meditations rising directly out of an incident or situation.

The narrator was ten years old when Mr. Coombs built the narrator's friend Malcolm his dream house:

> Pencil tucked behind his ear, Mr. Coombs
> bends over a beam bridging two inverted
> forty-gallon drums—its yellow fur erect, ready for
> the razor tongue of plane to shave its splinters,
> to peel its skin down to the smell of pine and pitch
> while Mr. Coombs up to his unlaced boots in clay
> whistles through gold-capped teeth, blessing with
> flicks of sweat the curtilage of Malcolm's plot.

When the house is finished they celebrate with a bottle of white rum and invite the boy in.

> Hardly listening to the drift
> of their post mortem, I choose the toolbox as my stool
> pondering the career of carpenters.

This is an enjoyable opening to a book of poems, and the enjoyment continues. The writing is full of accurately rendered and therefore interesting details. Reading *The Denting of a Wave* is like having a conversation with a friend who is intelligent and gifted with a sense of humor. It is not only a world that the poet builds us, but his life inside that world, from the opening poems about boyhood to his poetry of a grandfather. The subjects range from the one-room house in the bush to "Harbour View" . . . a view, I take it, of Kingston Harbour. This is one of the most perfectly realized poems in the book—perfectly because the poet refrains from trying to make anything grander and more significant of the scene than it is. The effect of the poem is in the composition, like a picture.

> Beyond the edge of my window
> overlooking the harbour
> the prow of a red cargo boat
> floats without motion
> on the blue water.

"But," he says, "it will not last." Either the ship will be "eaten up with demurrage," or it will sink or sail, or be driven onshore by wind and sea, "or I, unable to be a witness to defeat /

will close the curtain." The closing of the curtain closes the poem, making it one with the view.

Like all first-rate poetry, *The Denting of a Wave* demands something of the reader, and there are places where the writer's meaning is not as clear as it might be. But the general sense is always clear. Ralph Thompson speaks of himself as a "watcher of horizons" and a "hillside dweller," and his poetry has both breadth and height. But more than anything else perhaps, it is the voice of the writer that stays with you after you have closed the book: observant, knowledgeable about the world, and very entertaining.

There, They Could Say, Is the Jew

In 1741, Charles Macklin persuaded the Drury Lane Theater in London to put on *The Merchant of Venice*. Before Macklin it had been played for laughs, with a clowining Shylock. But Macklin had a new idea, and before the curtain went up the actors were apprehensive—they expected a disaster. The actress Kitty Clive, in the role of Portia, played her as a comic turn, with imitations of well-known lawyers of the day. But Macklin prevailed; he acted Shylock, in William Hazlitt's words, as "a decrepit old man, bent with age and ugly with mental deformity, grinning with deadly malice . . . fixed on one unalterable purpose, that of his revenge." The performance was a stunning success; Macklin would play Shylock for forty years.

In 1814, the strolling player Edmund Kean was engaged by Drury Lane and decided to make his debut as Shylock: "The Jew, or nothing!" His interpretation of the role would be, as John Gross tells us in *Shylock: A Legend and Its Legacy,* "one of the great theatrical legends of the century." Kean's style of acting, Hazlitt wrote, was pregnant with meaning, and the journalist W. J. Fox reported how Kean went about making it so: when Shylock said, "I would my daughter were dead at my foot, and the jewels in her ear! would she were hearsed at my foot, and the ducats in her coffin!" he started back "as with a revulsion of paternal feeling from the horrible image his avarice had conjured up." Kean's Shylock was still a malignant villain, but both critics and playgoers agreed that Kean's

---

Review of John Gross, *Shylock: A Legend and Its Legacy,* in *New York Times Book Review,* April 4, 1993.

achievement was to give Shylock a large measure of dignity and humanity.

So it would continue through the nineteenth century, audiences all over the world being thrilled by the malignancy and feeling for the man, to some extent.To feel too much for Shylock would have spoiled the fun; they were delighted to see him hoist by Portia with his own petard, the law. Villainy is good drama: when Shylock approached Antonio, knife in hand, to collect his pound of flesh, the audience was on the edge of its seat. The role, like those of Macbeth and Richard III, was a touchstone of acting.

But Shylock was larger than the play, larger than the theater. He is part of world mythology. His name is a verb in the dictionary: "To lend money at a high rate of interest." Shylock has been a subject for study by literary critics, psychoanalysts, and social historians. *The Merchant of Venice* was a favorite play of the Nazis; they seized upon it gleefully. "There," they could say, "is the Jew!"

John Gross is a former editor of the *Times Literary Supplement,* a former book critic of the *New York Times,* and now the drama critic of the *Sunday Telegraph* of London. His *Shylock* is not only a study of a literary masterpiece; it is also a study of history and of changing attitudes in the centuries since Shakespeare wrote. Shakespeare lived in a Christian world in which Jews were thought of as the people who rejected Christ. The Jews were expelled from England at the end of the thirteenth century. In the reign of Henry VIII some Jewish musicians arrived in England and were accepted in society. A colony of crypto-Jews, perhaps a hundred, existed in the reign of Elizabeth. In 1593 the Queen's physician, the Portuguese-born Roderigo (or Ruy) Lopez, was accused of trying to poison her at the instigation of the King of Spain. The prosecutor laid stress on Lopez being a Jew, "worse than Judas himself." Lopez was hanged, drawn and quartered at Tyburn.

This was what Shakespeare's audience knew about Jews. There had recently been a play by Christopher Marlowe, *The Jew of Malta,* that presented a monstrously evil Jew. When Shakespeare went to work, his first aim was to write a play for this audience. He was not the defender of oppressed Jews that some nineteenth- and twentieth-century liberals have wanted him to be. Shakespeare wasn't being ironic about the Christians in the play, didn't think of them as a set of idlers and hypocrites, as some current critics do.

Mr. Gross is incisive on this point: "We have been increasingly asked to think of 'The Merchant' as a play which cannot possibly mean what it appears to say. . . . Where the key words were once 'justice' and 'mercy,' 'gold' and 'love,' they are now (among others) 'skeptical,' 'tension,' 'discrepancy,' 'distancing' and "demystify.' " Mr. Gross speaks of the tone of the speeches that Shakespeare gives to Portia and Bassanio, Lorenzo and Jessica; it is romantic. The play is bathed in romance, as Portia's estate at Belmont is bathed in moonlight. "It is sometimes necessary to remind outselves," Mr. Gross remarks, "of the spirit of Shakespeare's plays. . . . Wholesale irony, running right through a play, is not Shakespeare's practice anywhere else." Mr. Gross's reading of Shakespeare drops on a wilderness of sophistry like the gentle rain from heaven.

So Shakespeare was writing about a villainous, usurious Jew. But he couldn't help writing with intelligence and imagination. To make Shylock merely a villain would not be nearly as good theater as if he were human too, with feelings that an audience could share. What would it be like to be Shylock? "I am a Jew. Hath not a Jew eyes? Hath not a Jew hands, organs, dimensions, senses, affections, passions? . . . If you prick us, do we not bleed?" Those actors in the footsteps of Kean who showed Shylock's humanity as well as his villainy, and who portrayed a tragic or sorely misused Shylock, may often, Mr. Gross says, "have gone too far, but it is Shakespeare himself who gave him their opening."

The anti-Semitism of Shakespeare's time was not like the anti-Semitism of ours. It was not a matter of blood but of belief. Shylock's daughter is accepted by the Christians at Belmont because she has dissociated herself from her father, and Antonio is willing to let Shylock keep half his property on certain conditions, one of which is that he will become a Christian. This is not the anti-Semitism of the twentieth century that machine-gunned Jews and threw them in pits, or herded Jewish men, women, and children to the gas chamber.

It is hardly possible to read *The Merchant of Venice* today without thinking of the abominations to which anti-Semitism, or any variety of racism, leads. Shakespeare's play, and other works of literature in which Jews were vilified, ranging from novels and detective stories to the poems of T. S. Eliot, contributed to anti-Semitism and made it socially acceptable. After the Holocaust one can hardly play *The Merchant of Venice* straight.

In 1970, when Laurence Olivier played Shylock at the National Theater in London, the scene was set in Victorian times and Shylock was a parvenu who tried to imitate the gentiles. In such a setting, the prospect of cutting a pound of flesh from Antonio was more grotesque than it could have seemed even to a sixteenth-century audience. The director, Jonathan Miller, played down the bond story and used burlesque stage business: "The song 'Tell Me Where Is Fancy Bred' was warbled," Mr. Gross writes, "by a pair of absurd Victorian sopranos, ogling at the lead casket to make sure Bassanio made the right choice." And so on.

Mr. Gross comments: "If I call Miller's 'Merchant' the key production of its period, it is not because it was necessarily the best, but because it was the one which established the principle that a director is free to do whatever he likes with the play—to bend it, twist it, advertise his boredom with it; to spice it up with anachronisms; to steamroller the poetry; to hit the audience over the head with what ought to be subtle implications. Virtually all Shakespeare's plays have been subjected to this kind of treatment in the past thirty years, but 'The Merchant of Venice,' given its subject matter, has proved an especially popular candidate."

In the 1960s and 1970s George Tabori produced *The Merchant of Venice,* first in America and then in Germany, as a play within a play: a group of concentration-camp prisoners is made to perform it to amuse their guards. "Tabori's target was Shakespeare as well as the Nazis—or rather, whatever it was in Shakespeare that enabled the Nazis to make use of him," Mr. Gross says. In a 1972 production by Peter Zadek in West Germany, Shylock was played as "a walking compendium of anti-Semitic clichés," in order to provoke the audience into examining its prejudices. Authors have used Shakespeare's characters in plays of their own. David Henry Wilson, in a preface to his play *Shylock's Revenge,* equates Shylock's intransigence with "the harsh intransigence of Israel." "The comparison between Israel and Shylock," Mr. Gross remarks, "seems to me profoundly unhelpful; but I suspect that it is one we may hear of again."

We hear these days about "interdisciplinary" studies. The idea is to bring different intellectual disciplines—literary criticism, history, philosophy, psychology, and sociology—to bear on a subject so as to light it from all sides. The trouble with such studies, when applied to literature, is that one discipline is frequently missing: an understanding of literature. John Gross's *Shylock* is an exception. Though he brings several viewpoints to bear on *The Merchant of Venice,* the play itself is his concern: a work that still has the power to move and delight.

It has always done so. Many of us saw it first when we were children, and I recall the excitement of watching Bassanio deciding which of the three caskets to choose—gold, silver, or lead—while we knew the answer. And the fascination with which we watched Shylock sharpening his knife—on the sole of his shoe, I seem to recall.

The Merchant of Venice is protean. The German poet Heine saw it as the conflict of Hellenism (Portia) versus Hebraism (Shylock). John Ruskin saw it as an episode in the history of socialism when anticapitalist and anti-Jewish themes were often entwined. C. S. Lewis thought it a fairy tale, and Frank Kermode reads it as allegorical. The critic M. C. Bradbrook remarked in 1951 that there were Shylocks as well as martyrs in the concentration camps, and seemed to be recommending forcible baptism for Jews who were criminals. The play brings all sorts of weird ideas out of the woodwork.

Freud, as you might expect, turned his attention to the play. In "The Theme of the Three Caskets" he examined the mythology of making a choice among three women, and concluded that in choosing one you opted for death. He had nothing to say, however, about Shylock. In 1921 the American psychoanalyst Isadore Coriat saw Shylock's usury as the result of forcible toilet training as a child; such people in later life, he thought, are unwilling "to deliver some very precious part of themselves." On the other hand, Theodore Reik and Robert Fleiss diagnosed Shylock as on oral type; he attacks with speech, his mouth.

With all that has been said about *The Merchant of Venice,* it still seems unexhausted, the character of Shylock as commanding and impenetrable as it was when Macklin or Kean, Edwin Booth, or Henry Irving held the stage. In *Shylock* John Gross has written an absorbing and lively study of this apparently timeless subject.

Irish Ghosts

Station Island is a sequence of dream encounters with familiar ghosts, set on Station Island on Lough Derg in Co. Donegal. The island is also known as St. Patrick's Purgatory because of a tradition that Patrick was the first to establish the penitential vigil of fasting and praying which still constitutes the basis of the three-day pilgrimage. Each unit of the contemporary pilgrim's exercises is called a "station," and a large part of each station involves walking barefoot and praying round the "beds," stone circles which are said to be the remains of early medieval monastic cells.

The note helps, especially if you are a foreigner, though many living in Ireland must be ignorant of Station Island and the exercises mentioned here. To Irish men and women of the kind called "educated," walking around the "beds" must seem as exotic as it does to me. And to a poet the pilgrimage to Station Island must not only seem exotic but antipoetic. Faith such as this has no need of poets; what these pilgrims think and do can only be marred by poetry. Faith is its own art and needs no other.

Why then is he here—a poet who has been to the university and traveled widely? From the evidence of his writing Seamus Heaney has no great love of religion, any more than he has of politics. He writes about Catholicism as he writes about the peat bogs—it is part of the landscape. But he is not, in the usual sense of the term, a religious poet.

Published in *Seamus Heaney: A Collection of Critical Essays,* ed. Elmer Andrews (London: Macmillan Press, 1992).

Are we to think that he has chosen the ritual at Station Island in the spirit that Shakespeare chose Oberon and his fairies, merely as a literary device? This was charming in Shakespeare—in Heaney it would be unforgivable, for people do believe in the exercises on Station Island, while Shakespeare's audience knew the play was only a dream. To take a ritual in which others believe and, without believing in it oneself, use it to make a poem, would be a lapse of taste and, what is more, intelligence. I don't suppose that anyone has ever accused Heaney of being unintelligent.

The answer, I think, is that without being the kind of person who would make the pilgrimage for religious reasons, Heaney is able to make it for personal reasons. And these are as heartfelt and sincere as if he were a true believer.

Yes, it is a literary device, and no, it is not just a device, but to be taken as an expression of the poet's sincere thought. The thought is so personal that he cannot handle it directly. It must be objectified, so he conceives it as a series of encounters with individuals, ideas seen as individuals. He has to deal with ghosts, and so do the people who fast and pray, so he will join their company, not because he believes in the things they believe, but because he feels as they do. He too is making a pilgrimage, and therefore he can be of the company.

Were all Chaucer's pilgrims religious? Each had his or her own reason for the exercise: it wasn't the reason that mattered, but the exercise. No one questioned the right of the Miller or the Pardoner to ride with the Nun. And Heaney has a right to walk behind the "crowd of shawled women."

But that he is not of them is shown at the start. He meets the ghost of "an old Sabbath-breaker," Simon Sweeney. Sweeney stands with a bow-saw that he holds "stiffly up like a lyre." "I was your mystery man," he says, "and am again this morning." Sweeney is not only a Sabbath-breaker, he is the spirit of poetry. To be a poet, it appears, is to break the Sabbath. As a child the narrator with his "First Communion face" would watch Sweeney through gaps in the bushes, cutting timber. Coming upon traces of Sweeney's handiwork in the woods he would feel "half afraid." On nights of wind and rain when they put him to bed with stories about tinkers, he would visualize Sweeney coming to get him. This morning as he prepares to join the pilgrims to Station Island, Sweeney shouts, "Stay clear of all processions!" The narrator will go with the pilgrims but he will believe in the "mystery man," Sweeney with his saw shaped like a lyre.

"Station Island" is about being a poet and the pilgrimage is to the source of the poet's creativity. But Heaney takes as his guide not Simon Sweeney, who stood in the child's mind for unlawful, Dionysiac behavior, but the poet of the *Inferno* and *Purgatorio*. Of the eleven sections of "Station Island," five are written in Dante's terza rima, and the tone is like Dante's, observant and restrained. The literary model helps Heaney to control his subject. He is going to speak of his feelings and, at the same time, public matters. In Dante as in Heaney, private and public life are mixed, the local and the general, the vernacular and "high" poetry. It is a daring thing to challenge comparison with Dante, but I do not think Heaney suffers by the comparison.

With the exception of terza rima, the forms of verse in "Station Island" seem to have been chosen for no particular reason. My guess would be that Heaney simply fell into writing the five-line stanzas in trimeter of the opening, the pentameter quatrains of Section III, the blank verse of Section V. And he seems to have rhymed when it pleased him.

The second apparition is that of William Carleton, author of *Traits and Stories of the Irish Peasantry,* who in his youth made the pilgrimage to Lough Derg. The poet is sitting in a parked car when Carleton appears striding along the road. Carleton is an angry man, fed up with the politics of both Ribbonmen and Orangemen. He thinks there's "something natural" about the poet's smile, but something defensive too. The poet replies that he has "no mettle for the angry role." His memories of the Ribbonmen are their hymns to Mary, "obedient strains," and he felt no sympathy for the "harp of unforgiving iron / the Fenians strung." He has shared Carleton's experiences, "flax-pullings, dances, summer crossroads chat." He speaks of his local education, of Orange drums and "neigh-bours on the roads at night with guns."

"I know," Carleton says, and tells him to "try to make sense of what comes. / Remember everything and keep your head." The narrator speaks of things that have mattered to him, ranging from mushrooms to "old jampots in a drain clogged up with mud." Carleton interrupts:

> "All this is like a trout kept in a spring
> or maggots sown in wounds—
> another life that cleans our element."

I interpret "All this" to mean the totality of "what comes." This would fit with his parting words:

> "We are earthworms of the earth, and all that
> has gone through us is what will be our trace."

Carleton disappears up the road. He stands for flax-pullings and old jampots, and against abstractions.

If Heaney is not religious, why is he kneeling? He gives an answer: "Habit's afterlife." The third section of "Station Island" takes us back to the atmosphere of a church,

> an active wind-stilled hush, as if
> in a shell the listened-for ocean stopped
> and a tide rested and sustained the roof.

He recalls a toy grotto covered with shells and cockles, "that housed the snowdrop weather of her death." He remembers the prayer for the sick that was said in church and how as he prayed he thought of death as "a space utterly empty, / utterly a source like the idea of sound." It was also their dog that disappeared weeks before, "the bad carcass and scrags of hair" found in a swamp.

If we wonder why Heaney is making the stations, he asks the question himself through the voice of a priest, one he knew as a clerical student, "home for the summer / doomed to the decent thing," who reassured the parishioners in their outmoded faith. Later he served on foreign missions.

> "And you," he faltered, "what are you doing here
> but the same thing? What possessed you?
> I at least was young and unaware
>
> that what I thought was chosen was convention.
> But all this you were clear of you walked into
> over again. And the god has, as they say, withdrawn."

He suggests that the poet my be "here taking a last look"—that is, may have come to Lough Derg out of nostalgia to observe a vanishing custom. The poet neither affirms nor denies this explanation.

We now meet three apparitions who were the poet's teachers: Barney Murphy, who taught Latin at the Anahorish School; an unnamed master with a liking for quotations and an eye for detail; and the poet Patrick Kavanagh. Kavanagh is as humorous and satiric in death as he was in life—Heaney has caught the tone exactly. Kavanagh made the journey to "Station Island," and he mocks the narrator for following in his footsteps.

> "Sure I might have known
> once I had made the pad, you'd be after me
> sooner or later."

—and ends with an insult:

> "In my own day
> the odd one came here on the hunt for women."

Learning, an eye for detail, and humor—these are the gifts of Heaney's masters. The learning is obvious, and the details are inserted so easily that one takes them for granted. But they account for much of the power of Heaney's writing, his ability to convince. They appear in metaphors and, as they are usually homely details, convince us that the thing being said is true. The name of the dead missionary is "like an old bicycle wheel in a ditch / ripped at last from under jungling briars," and Barney Murphy's "Adam's apple in its weathered sac / worked like the plunger of a pump in drought." These details make it possible to believe in the apparitions. As for humor, I hardly need to point out that there is plenty of it in Heaney's writing, and satire whose edge is so subtle that it is hardly felt. Consider the second teacher and his love of quotation:

> *"For what is the great*
> *moving power and spring of verse? Feeling, and*
> *in particular, love."*

There's nothing wrong with the idea, and I think Heaney would agree with it in general, but the way of saying it carries it over into the ridiculous. One wishes to throw something, if only a piece of chalk, at the teacher.

Kavanagh's remark about women brings us to a sexual episode of the narrator's childhood: "her I chose at 'secrets' / And whispered to." I suppose that "secrets" is like the games boys and girls play in other places that lead to kissing. The boy in the poem was sexually frustrated, "Mad for it, and all that ever opened / Was the breathed-on grille of a confessional." But the freckled girl of the poem showed him "the wheatlands of her back" and he "inhaled the land of kindness."

This is innocent and happy—we seem to be reading an Irish version of *Tom Sawyer*. But we are in for a shock: this innocence is followed by murder. The scenes are placed side by side for maximum shock, so that we may feel the contrasts of Irish life, tenderness on the one hand, violence on the other. Section VII deals with the political situation Irish men and women have to think about every day of their lives, and the violence it causes. I have said that the poetry of "Station Island" is both personal and public, and here we see why it is so: the murdered shopkeeper was well known to the poet. There must be many in Ireland who have seen such apparitions.

The poet's feelings are clear: like Yeats he is against fanaticism and the use of violence. But it is not a simple thing to hold this attitude: there are those in Ireland, as throughout the world, who believe that violence is necessary in order to arrive at justice of one sort or another. It appears that a solution cannot be arrived at by arguing—the arguments go back for centuries and are tangled and knotted, it seems, beyond anyone's ability to untie them. Instead of arguing, let us see. . . .

When I said that passages in "Station Island" bear comparison with Dante's *Inferno* and *Purgatorio*, it was Section VII I had in mind particularly. In this part all Heaney's powers come together, his realism, his attention to detail, his narrative ability, and his powers of feeling. It absorbs us so that we forget we are reading—we are living more intensely. The poem spoken by the murdered man is not at all self-pitying or sentimental, and this makes us feel that it is true. The knocking at the door, the "whingeing and screeching" of the wife, his shouting at her, this is how such things must happen. At the end, the poet says,

> "Forgive the way I have lived indifferent—
> forgive my timid circumspect involvement,"

to which the spirit answers,

> "Forgive
> my eye . . . all that's above my head."

So the poet broaches what most concerns him, his "timid circumspect involvement," and I think that the answer, "all that's above my head," is his as well as the ghost's. All the poet can do is serve as a witness, and he does so convincingly:

> And then a stun of pain seemed to go through him
>
> and he trembled like a heatwave and faded.

From the reality of this scene, as close to flesh and blood as words can make it, "Station Island" slopes down to the end. Not that the writing is less good, but it is less like a thing experienced and more like meditation and praying. This, of course, is in keeping with the background movement, walking and kneeling by the "beds."

In Section VIII, as he kneels at St. Brigid's Bed, the poet sees the ghost of an Irish archaeologist who died young. Their talk culminates in a vision of axe heads, "a cairn of stone force," violence going back for centuries, and, opposing this, the plaster cast of an abbess the archaeologist once gave him, "mild-mouthed and cowled, a character of grace." But this nicely balanced composition yields, once more, to the vision of a murdered man. He is the poet's cousin, and appears to be the shop-keeper of Section VII. He accuses the poet of indifference:

> "You were there with poets when you got the word
> and stayed there with them, while your own flesh and blood
> was carted to Bellaghy from the Fews.
> They showed more agitation at the news
> than you did."

The poet tries to defend himself. Those others "happened in on / live sectarian assassination," while he was overwhelmed by a sense of destiny.

> "I kept seeing a grey stretch of Lough Beg
> and the strand empty at daybreak.
> I felt like the bottom of a dried-up lake."

This explanation doesn't wash—the murdered man still accuses him:

> "You saw that, and you wrote that—not the fact.
> You confused evasion and artistic tact."

He accuses his Protestant murderer directly, and the poet indirectly, for having drawn "the lovely blinds of the *Purgatorio* / and saccharined my death with morning dew." So the poet accuses himself and his poem written in Dante's terza rima. But I do not think that we have to agree with this criticism—taking Dante as a model has not drawn "lovely blinds":

> I turned to meet his face and the shock
>
> is still in me at what I saw. His brow
> was blown open above the eye and blood
> had dried on his neck and cheek. "Easy now,"

he said, "it's only me. You've seen men as raw
after a football match . . ."

A hostel is the setting for Section IX. The poet dreams that
he is a gunman who was caught, imprisoned, and executed by
a firing squad. This nightmare is followed by a dream of a
"mucky, glittering flood" in which

> Strange polyp floated like a huge corrupt
> Magnolia bloom, surreal as a shed breast, . . .

It is the image of his "softly awash and blanching self-
disgust"—disgust at his own life that "kept me competent /
To sleepwalk with connivance and mistrust." But then a lighted
candle rises out of the polyp, showing the course and cur-
rents, and

> No more adrift,
> My feet touched bottom and my heart revived.

Then a round, clear, "mildly turbulent" object rises in a
"cobwebbed space"—a trumpet, so close and brilliant that he
falls backward, and he wakes to the sound of the bell in the
hostel dormitory.

> Still there for the taking!
> The old brass trumpet with its valves and stops
> I found once in loft thatch, a mystery
> I shied from then for I thought such trove beyond me.

Like Simon Sweeney in the opening part, the trumpet
speaks for poetry itself, which the poet feels he has be-
trayed. As he faces himself shaving in the mirror he de-
spises himself for being so "biddable and unforthcoming."
Yet it seems he had no more power to change things than
an eddy in a pool or a stone in a cascade. But this is fol-
lowed by a thought:

> Then I thought of the tribe whose dances never fail
> For they keep dancing till they sight the deer.

144

Section X, which is also set in the hostel, strikes me as the weak poem in the series, perhaps because the poet here comes close to adopting a traditional, reverential position. It goes against the grain of the rest of "Station Island," which, as I said earlier, derives its strength from the poet's unconventionality—he is on the pilgrimage for a personal rather than a religious reason. In Section X he remembers an earthenware mug that stood on a shelf beyond his reach. It was once used in a play and "glamoured from this translation." This brings to mind Ronan's psalter, which was lost in a lough and brought to the surface by an otter:

> And so the saint praised God on the lough shore.
> The dazzle of the impossible suddenly
> blazed across the threshold, a sun-glare
> to put out the small hearths of constancy.

I have said that Heaney is not a religious poet. This poem might make one think otherwise—and I may be mistaken. But I do not think so, and the conclusion of "Station Island" bears me out.

In Section XI a priest appears who once told the poet, "Read poems as prayers . . . and for your penance / translate me something by Juan de la Cruz." The translation follows:

> How well I know that fountain, filling, running,
>   although it is the night.
>
> That eternal fountain, hidden away,
> I know its haven and its secrecy
>   although it is the night.
>
> But not its source because it does not have one,
> which is all sources' source and origin
>   although it is the night.

This poet, in the dark night of Irish politics, has found the consolation other poets have found, the belief in a reality that is not of this world. It happens to coincide with a religious view of reality, and may be confused with it, but there is a difference: poets believe they are creating reality, whereas priests teach that it has been revealed. Heaney takes his place in a line of poets from Baudelaire to the present who are competing with religion—their god is poetry, not the God of priests and saints.

This is made clear in the conclusion, where the poet returns from Station Island to the mainland, feeling like a convalescent. A hand stretches down from the jetty to help him ashore. It is the hand of a master:

> the tall man in step at my side
> seemed blind, though he walked straight as a rush
> upon his ash plant . . .

He is the author of *Ulysses,* and we are not surprised to hear him say,

> "Your obligation
> is not discharged by any common rite.
> What you must do must be done on your own
>
> so get back in harness. The main thing is to write
> for the joy of it. . . ."

Nor are we surprised when he says, "let others wear the sackcloth and the ashes," nor when he has this to say on the question of whether the poet should write in English or Irish:

> "Who cares,"
> he jeered, "any more? The English language
> belongs to us. You are raking at dead fires,
>
> a waste of time for somebody your age.
> That subject people stuff is a cod's game,
> infantile, like your peasant pilgrimage.
>
> You lose more of yourself than you redeem
> doing the decent thing."

His advice to the poet is to write and:

> "fill the element
> with signatures on your own frequency,
> echo soundings, searches, probes, allurements."

This is in keeping with the words of Stephen Dedalus: "Welcome, O life! I go to encounter for the millionth time the reality of experience and to forge in the smithy of my soul the uncreated conscience of my race." As I have said, these poets are competing with the Church—poetry is their religion.

Can you only be concerned with poetry when the people around you are engaged in political action? Shouldn't you take an active part? Heaney dramatizes the question and lets the drama find its own, aesthetic solution. Presenting matters of conscience in the form of a narrative makes them seem fictional and gives the author the absolution he seeks. "Station Island" marks a crisis in Heaney's thinking, discharging a cloud of dark thoughts that have been gathering for some time. If he has been criticized for having only, in his own words, a "timid circumspect involvement," "Station Island" defends his position and, I think, does so admirably.

A review in the *Times Literary Supplement* states that Heaney believes that poetry in the West is failing for want of the "governing power" he finds in the poetry of Eastern Europe.[1] If this is what Heaney really believes, writing "Station Island" has not put his doubts to rest. I do not think that a true poet ever stops questioning his motives, and it is tempting for a writer to let politics take over and do his thinking for him. But poetry is not failing as long as poets write about what they know and, in the words of the ghost, write for the joy of it.

---

1. See Edward Mendelson, "Poetry as Fate and Faith," review of Seamus Heaney's *The Government of the Tongue*, in *Times Literary Supplement*, July 1, 1988, p. 726.

An American View of Pasternak

No American poet, with the possible exception of Robert Frost, has meant as much to his countrymen as Boris Pasternak has meant to his. There are poets in the United States who have taken a stand on public matters. The best known is Allen Ginsberg; he is a minor celebrity, the only poet whose name rings a bell with the general public. Among our women poets, Adrienne Rich stands out as a feminist, that is, one who speaks from a female point of view. There are dozens of American poets who make frequent public appearances, reading their poems to an audience and expressing their opinions. But of all these poets not one carries the weight of Boris Pasternak, who for most of his creative life was withdrawn from events and lived in obscurity. He was not compelled to be obscure—he preferred to be. He wrote:

> Plunge then into obscurity
> Concealing in it every pace

The essay has a curious provenance. A Russian telephoned from Manhattan. He wanted an essay on Pasternak for a magazine in Moscow, *Literaturnaya Gazeta,* and he wanted it right away, for it would be published on Pasternak's anniversary and he had to translate my English into Russian before the deadline. I hastened to oblige and my wife traveled to the city and delivered the essay at his hotel. I telephoned him to ask if he had received it and he said that he had. This was the last we heard of him or my essay. The affair is cloaked in mystery. Is there a black market for literary criticism in Russia?

Just as the landscape disappears
Into the fog, and leaves no trace.[1]

But Pasternak has left traces in the writings of younger poets such as Andrei Voznesensky and in the consciousness of all readers of poetry.

How can this be? How is it that a man who lived apart, who in his writings scarcely spoke about the events of his time, and then only in indirect, riddling terms, could be felt by his contemporaries to be the one, above all, who spoke for them? During the years of his obscurity, before *Doctor Zhivago*, people knew that Pasternak was *there*, a presence among them, and conjectured what he must be thinking. The empty chair was the one on which all eyes were fixed.

The answer is in Pasternak's own words: "One must live in sovereign freedom like a king, never surrendering to temporal authority or traditions, however, deeply rooted, but out of one's own acquired perfections in complete honesty."[2] He turned away from the events, and chaos, of the times in order to perfect his art. He was attacked virulently in some quarters for doing so by those who had taken the opposite direction. But others sensed that Pasternak's art was in the service of life . . . any life that would survive the chaos. He was giving them bread while those others were giving them stones.

As I have said, the same quality has been perceived in the life and work of the American poet, Robert Frost, and this may be why he was invited to visit the Soviet Union. There are other American poets who have the strength of the "acquired perfections in complete honesty" that Pasternak urged, but on a smaller scale. Among women poets, Denise Levertov . . . among the men, Robert Bly. They have written well, but no book that has struck their contemporaries as powerfully as

---

1. "It's Unbecoming," in Boris Pasternak, *In the Interlude: Poems 1945–1960,* trans. Henry Kamen (London: Oxford University Press, 1962), pp. 104, 105.

2. Cited by Phillip C. Flayderman in Boris Pasternak, *Sister My Life,* trans. Phillip C. Flayderman (New York: Washington Square Press, 1967), pp. x, xi.

Sister My Life. One might say that they are not as gifted as Pasternak and let it go at that. But I think it is not so simple: to know why poets in the United States do not carry the weight that they do in Russia, and in fact do not see themselves as very important, one would have to examine the differences between the two countries, their history and culture. "In Russia," a Russian poet once told me, "our poets are as important as your senators. In Moscow when two or three poets meet for an evening, the next day everyone wants to know what they talked about, what they decided." It is certainly different in the United States. The words of our poets have no weight with the people at large, or with the government.

An apparent exception: during the war in Vietnam, several American poets spoke publicly against the war. The poet Robert Lowell, when invited to the White House, refused to go as a protest against the war. A number of American poets, of whom I was one, wrote to the president in support of Lowell's stand. This angered Lyndon Johnson greatly, but such protests had an effect—they were instrumental in convincing Johnson that the war could not be brought to a successful conclusion. They contributed in no small measure to limiting the war and preventing it from becoming worse than it was . . . which was bad enough. But the poets who stood with Lowell were not influencing anyone through their poetry— they were acting as citizens who, because they were poets, happened for a moment to be in the limelight.

The case of Pasternak was very different. He did not take part in demonstrations or protests, he only wrote . . . poems. And a large number of the poems were about nature, or seemed to be. Yet he was able to influence his countrymen strongly and, if reports are to be believed, impressed Stalin. He must have, otherwise he would probably have shared the fate of Mandelstam.

Let us, then, speak of Pasternak's poetry, for the secret of his power is there. I have made a list comparing the poetry of Pasternak with American poetry, describing those aspects of Pasternak in which I think he is superior and two aspects in which I think he is wanting.

Points of Pasternak's superiority:

(1) his sense of his unique destiny as a poet, the urgency of his vocation, which made him put all his intelligence and energy into the actual writing. He wasn't a part-time poet as so many American poets are. American poets seem to lack real ambition, as one of them, Donald Hall, has pointed out. Perhaps they lack faith in the reality of the written word. From their beginnings as a nation, Americans have placed a premium on the ability of a man or woman to *do* something—this was what was needed . . . the ability to use an axe or do business. And they have regarded the arts as useless.

(2) Pasternak's spontaneous and deep feelings, first expressed in *Sister My Life*. Feeling is essential—without it, poetry cannot be "great." This is what people want from poetry, and they don't often find it in American poems. Walt Whitman showed the way, but few have followed. I do not regard the so-called "confessional" poets, writers such as Anne Sexton, as poets of feeling, for what they express is more often hysteria than feeling. I mean feeling that communicates to others, on a deep level, the life we all share.

(3) Pasternak's idea of nature. In this lies his originality, and it carries over from nature into his view of human life. In his early poems nature is a power acting upon humanity, not merely reflecting human thoughts as it does in weak Romantic poetry. I emphasize "weak" because in strong Romantic poetry such as Wordsworth's and Whitman's, nature is shown as embodying a mind and will of its own. Pasternak's strictures on Romanticism are aimed at poets who merely fantasize, whose poetry is not rooted in life. His involvement with nature accounts for his style . . . its liveliness, its colloquialisms, its cleaving to the ways in which people actually think and speak. That these ways are sometimes fantastic is to be expected. But the poet himself is not a fantasist—he is the medium of a truth.

It is hard to find, outside Whitman and Robert Frost, an American poet who loves nature with the intensity of Pasternak. In his poetry, as Sinyavsky and other critics have remarked, nature behaves like a person.

The mist from everywhere comes flooding like a sea,
Trailing its stockings on thistles . . .[3]

and

The raindrops seemed to kick at doors
And it smelled outdoors like a wine cork.[4]

There is no distancing or barrier in Pasternak between humankind and nature. In fact, he thinks through nature; that is, in his poetry things are seen from the point of view of the mist and the raindrops. "The poetry and prose of the late Pasternak," Sinyavsky writes, "unexpectedly shift his vision to a different realm—that of philosophical and metaphysical thought which his earlier verse appeared not to enter."[5] But this shift did not entail a reversal; Pasternak continued to think through and like nature to the end.

I have recently come across a poem by an American that, I think, is as fine as any poem about nature written by Pasternak. It is by Robert Bly, whom I have mentioned. But writing such as this is all too rare in our literature.

Gnats

This cloud of gnats resembles
ghost substance—
it changes
shape, lifts or sinks.

They are too excited—
they can't be feeding.
So few days to live
and they spend it this way![6]

---

3. "The Steppe," *Sister My Life,* pp. 88, 89.
4. "Summer," *Sister My Life,* pp. 130, 131.
5. Andrey Sinyavsky, "Pasternak's Poetry," In *Pasternak: A Collection of Critical Essays,* ed. Victor Erlich (Englewood Cliffs, N.J.: Prentice-Hall, 1978), p. 101.
6. Robert Bly, *The Apple Found in the Plowing* (Baltimore and Philadelphia: Haw River Books, 1989), n.p.

(4) Among Pasternak's points of superiority is his love of women. I do not know why there is so little of this in American poetry. Perhaps it is because women and nature are intimately related, and Americans have been fighting nature since the days of the pioneers. Americans were born "against nature," they had to create themselves. Many an American has been created, as Scott Fitzgerald says of the Great Gatsby, out of a Platonic concept of himself. In any case, Americans have not written much love poetry. Perhaps things are changing now that American women in increasing numbers are writing poetry. It may be that when we have an Akhmatova, American poets will fall in love with the idea of the American woman. Perhaps they will be able to write with the tenderness and humor of Boris Pasternak:

> And then I sulkily had to endure
> Lash-like the women prattling without end;
> So loving them thereafter was a science,
> Adoring them, a feat, to comprehend.[7]

On two points I do not think Pasternak has anything to say to American poets. The first is the didacticism that appears from time to time in his writing, in lines such as

> Don't sleep, don't sleep, keep working,
> Don't cease work for one hour . . .[8]

This strikes me as very old-fashioned. To find its like in American poetry one would have to go back to the writings of Longfellow in the nineteenth century. These moralizings and exhortations are like the well-meaning but intrusive voice of Polonius. When Pasternak writes like this he seems as inferior to his true self, the poet of imagination, as Polonius is to Hamlet.

The other point is Pasternak's rejection of "formal experiments." He said, "I have never understood those dreams of a

---

7. "Women in Childhood," *In the Interlude: Poems 1945–1960,* pp. 210, 211.

8. "Night," *In the Interlude: Poems 1945–1960,* pp. 150, 151.

new language, of a completely original form of expression. Because of this dream, much of the work of the twenties was merely stylistic experimentalism and has ceased to exist. The most extraordinary discoveries are made when the artist is overwhelmed by what he has to say. In his urgency he uses the old language, and the old language is transformed from within."[9]

This is where I, and others like me, part company with Pasternak. From its real beginnings in the poems of Whitman, who said that *Leaves of Grass* was a "language experiment," American poetry has had a tradition of "formal experiments." The great American poems, Whitman's "Song of Myself" and T. S. Eliot's *The Waste Land,* are experiments in form. There have been American poets who continued to write, in the manner of traditional English verse, in rhyme and meter, and the remark of Robert Frost is well known: he said that he'd as soon try to play tennis without a net as write free verse. At the present moment there is a movement afoot in the United States to write again in the "traditional," that is, old English manner: there are poets who wish to write quatrains and sestinas. But their nostalgia for fixed forms has not produced poetry of any note. The mainstream of American writing, as of American life, is "formal experiment." The words of Emerson almost a hundred and fifty years ago marked the course that American poetry would take. He said, "It is not metres, but a metre-making argument that makes a poem—a thought so passionate and alive that like the spirit of a plant or an animal it has an architecture of its own, and adorns nature with a new thing." It is regrettable that Boris Pasternak, whose thought was so passionate and alive, when he spoke of the forms of verse threw the weight of his critical opinion on the side of "the old language." In everything else he was ahead of his time, and for all time.

---

9. Cited by Olga Andreyev Carlisle in Boris Pasternak, *My Sister, Life and Other Poems,* ed. and trans. Olga Andreyev Carlisle (New York and London: Harcourt Brace Jovanovich, 1976), p. 13.

Thoughts about a
Doubtful Enterprise

What is the use of poetry? Is it of any use at all in the modern world? Robert Frost once expressed himself on this subject in a letter.

> You wish the world better than it is, more poetical. You are that kind of poet. I would rate as the other kind. I wouldn't give a cent to see the world, the United States, or even New York, made better. I want them left just as they are for me to make—poetical on paper.

I think Frost's point of view may be incomprehensible to many people, including writers and teachers. As Edgar Allen Poe said long ago and Baudelaire would say after him, Americans want art to be morally uplifting. In our schools young people are taught that poetry has a message. No wonder that outside of school they never look at a poem. Poetry is too exquisitely boring.

What people who want art to be morally uplifting do not see is that in putting art to an immediate use they prevent it from exercising its real function, waking and enlarging the imagination. They do not see that the apparent selfishness and indifference to social causes of a poet such as Frost is in the service of the artist's work, which, if it is any good at all, must appeal to others, and so is not selfish. The more dedicated the artist is to

Talk given at Hampden-Sydney College, November 8, 1990, on being awarded the degree of Doctor of Letters. Published in the *Hampden-Sydney Poetry Review,* Winter 1991.

his work, the more he contributes to society. He is surrounded by people who urge him to do this, to do that, some thing that cries out to be done. But no voice except his own is urging him to paint the picture or write the poem, and this is the voice he must listen to if he is to do his work.

There have been periods of civilization when the artist's inner voice and the voices of society were one: when Aeschylus, Sophocles, and Euripides wrote for a public theater, when artists were commissioned to decorate the churches of Italy, when a novel by Dickens appeared in a magazine in monthly installments. But we are not living in such a period of civilization now. The general public knows nothing of art—it doesn't know what it likes. The public hopes that a committee of experts, appointed by the state, will tell it what art is. And millions of Americans do not read a book from one end of the year to the other. I am not speaking of the poor who have had no means of getting an education: I am speaking of supposedly educated people.

Is it necessary for people to be readers? It is, if ever they are to express their own feelings and ideas . . . in fact, if they are to have ideas. The pathetic sentences of American students when they are compelled to write, as though they were being tortured, show the connection between thinking and reading: they do not read, therefore they do not think.

But why read something as special as poetry? Isn't it just a luxury? Suppose the young person were educated in science; wouldn't that be better than reading poetry that, as we know, has nothing to do with life? No, I'm afraid a scientific education isn't enough; science and the psuedosciences are built on theories, and these become useless and have to be replaced. But there is nothing as real and lasting as a poem: it begins with our sense-perceptions, with what we see and hear, what we imagine we could touch, or taste, or smell. Not with the senses themselves, for these are ephemeral, but our imagining of the senses, which is not ephemeral. Poetry has its body in words, which pass from the life of the individual to the life of others and to lives in the next generation. The plays of Shakespeare are still with us and are acted every day. His words affect us by waking our dormant senses. Through his words we are able to feel again what the people of his time were feeling when they went to the theater. But where is the science of Shakespeare's time? As dead as a doornail.

I shall quote Frost again—he is very quotable. He said, "My poems are the unforced expression of a life I was forced to live." If this is true, there could be nothing more real than the poetry such a person would write.

A life he was forced to live. This is the sense of life that poets have. I mean true poets, not just those who publish lines of verse—as Ben Jonson said, "A rhymer, and a *poet,* are two things"—I mean those who write the poems we remember. When we read their poems we are conscious of a life that had to be lived in a certain way. It is this that gives their writing its authority. With this sense of a special destiny goes the sense of having to express it in certain ways. Just writing down what you feel won't do. The feeling has to be expressed in a definite form, in certain words and no other.

An illusion, you may think. Besides, no one thinks in such terms nowadays. The word "destiny" is hopelessly old-fashioned. At least I might have used the language of psychology and spoken of a compulsion. Yes, and that would have put poetry in its place as a kind of nervous disorder. But if poets think like psychologists and sociologists they will lose the sense I have been speaking of, the sense of dedication. They become mere puppets of scientific theory. It is necessary for poets not to bow before the idols of the marketplace but to stick to their sense of reality. Let them stick to expressing their thoughts in images and writing in lines, even rhyming if they must. For the forms of writing are intimately related to their perceptions, and through their perceptions to real ideas. As Locke remarked, and Aristotle before him, "There cannot be an idea that has not first been perceived through the senses."

It all depends on us, on our perceptions and our sense of the importance of what we ourselves have perceived. I have never understood Whitman's saying that to have great poetry there must be great audiences too. If by great he meant big audiences, nothing could be less true: it wouldn't apply to Whitman's own poetry, for he had no audience to speak of when he was writing his poems: they were better received abroad than in his own beloved States. I think he may have meant by "great audiences" people who are great readers, who have the root of the matter in them. You don't need many friends—a few are enough, maybe only one or two. What audience did Emily Dickinson have, or Elizabeth Bishop? I do not think that the poet need think of an audience at all. But let us say that these are exceptional cases and that, for most poets, it would be encouraging to have an audience. The reason that the writers and artists of Renaissance Italy are famous throughout the world is that they worked for a few people who had a highly developed sense of aesthetics, and beyond these a public capable of judging poetry and art. But the American poet or artist is not in that situation. She is lucky if she can reach an audience of a few hundred.

A poet who has a considerable reputation—among poets, that is—recently said to me, "I am doubtful about the whole enterprise." He meant, the enterprise of writing poetry in the United States. I could share his feeling. Poems are published in magazines that very few people read. Books of poetry are published and drop out of sight, unreviewed and, it seems, unread. What poet has not felt that people have stopped reading verse? And what's the use of writing if no one reads? Teachers, I think, may be more apprehensive than most, for they have seen the decline of reading up close. The side of me that teaches is troubled by this—but the side that writes not at all. For I am sure that out there, among the great non-poetry-reading, television-watching public, there is a handful of readers. What more can one ask for? Would one like to be a best-selling poet like Rod McKuen? Why would anyone want to have a large public? As far as I am concerned, Emily Dickinson said the final word on the subject.

> How dreary to be somebody!
> How public, like a frog
> To tell your name the livelong day
> To an admiring bog!

Having no public didn't hurt Emily Dickinson. Ah, you may say, but think what she might have done if there had been "an audience for poetry." Yes, what she wrote might have been different . . . perhaps more like the poetry of Longfellow, more facile and far less memorable.

I think we should not be concerned that poetry does not have a large audience. It is in the nature of poetry to appeal only to those who feel a need for it, who are passionately fond of words moving in rhythm, of sound and sense moving together. Those who can hear this music are blessed, and they have always been a minority. It was so in Chaucer's time—and he, incidentally, thought the enterprise might be failing, that the language in which he wrote was changing and there might come a day when no one would be able to read and understand the lines on which he spent so much care, brooding over them by night in his room above the gate after his day's work in the Customs, counting bundles of wool and keeping an eye peeled for sharp practice. But we are reading Chaucer today, and there are some who read him more carefully than any reader in his own lifetime.

Let us not exaggerate. It is as sentimental to think that poetry is dying as to think that thousands of people should welcome a book of verse with joyful cries. Those who read poems are a minority, but what a minority! They may not fill a plaza or have their picture on the society page of the *Times*, but the enterprise on which they have embarked is likely to last as long as the human race itself. This was good enough for Wordsworth, for Keats, for Whitman, Eliot, Pasternak, and dozens of other poets and their readers. If you are a poet or reader of poetry, it should be enough for you. Your job is to be good enough for it.

We don't have to worry about the future of poetry: poems will be written as long as poets are born. But for those who don't want to leave the matter entirely to chance, who want to do something, I have a practical suggestion. Do you want to be a poet? Then teach. Reading has to be kept up. There are those who would like to be poets and don't know how to go about it, how they are to shape their lives to that end. Let them become teachers. If they are destined to be poets they will be; in the meantime, by teaching poetry they will be doing a great deal of good. People with a love of poetry are desperately needed at the present time in departments of English, languages, and comparative literature, for those departments are being taken over by those who have no love of literature. Indeed, as they have proudly and repeatedly proclaimed, they wish to use literature only as a means of demonstrating critical theories. Jacques Derrida and Paul de Man had no respect for authors; in fact, they told us that authors are irrelevant. It is language that writes, not an author. Stanley Fish tells us that the aim of teaching is to advance oneself in the profession. The followers of these successful theorists are even less attached to literature; Derrida, de Man, and Fish had at least read the authors they set out to deconstruct, but these have only read critical theory. They are like the followers of Marx who do not take into account the results of Marxism in practice. Perfecting a theory is all that matters: whether or not it can be applied concerns them not at all.

> Enough of such as for their bellies' sake,
> Creep and intrude and climb into the fold!
> Of other care they little reckoning make,
> Than how to scramble at the shearers' feast,
> And shove away the worthy bidden guest;
> Blind mouths! that scarce themselves know how to hold
> A sheep hook . . .

It is certain that deconstructionists have never held a sheep hook, that they don't know the first thing about writing, why anyone would want to write a poem or story. Meanwhile, the hungry sheep look up and are not fed—they are deserting the humanities in flocks. Therefore, let those who like poetry so well that they want to write it be teachers. They needn't be afraid that studying and having to impart what they have learned to others will spoil their writing. It could make them better, because more knowledgeable, writers.

Here I must say something about courses in creative writing. They are often taught by writers who do not care about literature and who encourage their students to express themselves in any way they can. The writing so produced is of little interest. If these teachers were not just writers but teachers of literature, they might encourage their students to have ideas and show them how to write in a variety of forms. Then what they wrote might be of some interest outside the classroom.

You may recall the remark of Robert Frost's with which I began: "I wouldn't give a cent to see the world, the United States, or even New York made better." This seems a very antisocial statement. Some of you may have thought, "That's why no one cares about poetry. It's useless." It is strange, isn't it, that the poems of the man who made that statement are found in schoolbooks and in American homes, and have been translated into foreign languages. Why has the writing of such an unsocial person been so widely accepted?

Because it is real: it is the United States, and the world, and even New York. This is where reality is, and there is no other. The rest is just houses, streets, and buildings. Without poetry there is no society. The Bible puts it better: "Where there is no vision the people perish." Why should Frost have cared about the illusions that society provides so amply when he was at work creating the real world, the one we carry in our heads and future generations will carry, if they carry anything at all?

The writer Joseph Conrad, who was a poet though in prose, spoke of the greater society to which poets belong:

> My task which I am trying to achieve is, by the power of the written word to make you hear, to make you feel—it is, before all, to make you *see*. . . . In a single-minded attempt of that kind . . . one may perchance attain to such clearness of sincerity that at last the presented vision of regret or pity, of terror or mirth, shall awaken in the hearts of the beholders that feeling of unavoidable solidarity; of the solidarity in mysterious origin, in toil, in joy, in hope, in uncertain fate, which binds men to each other and all mankind to the visible world.

Conrad adds that the writer who holds this conviction "cannot be faithful to any one of the temporary formula of his craft," meaning that he cannot subscribe to a partisan way of thinking and writing: he must bring to his work everything he knows. Conrad is asking of the writer nothing less than his life. I shall add that work done in this spirit depends to a certain extent on chance, as does life itself. A misstep to this side or that, and pouff . . . it goes up in smoke. Think how many who shared Conrad's faith in solidarity and the use of words have perished unheard, because chance was against them. The fear of the Lord, the Bible tells us, is the beginning of wisdom. It is also the beginning of our sense of the precariousness of life, the importance of words, and our need to write them truly.

Whole civilizations have perished leaving only a handful of words. If those of you who write poetry, and those who read it, feel that the enterprise is failing, consider that it is, nevertheless, the only enterprise on which human beings can count. Numbers don't seem to matter, nor do reinforced concrete or military weapons. Those who congratulate themselves on being in the majority of those who don't care about poetry or art or religion should consider the history of Hitler's Germany and Stalin's Russia. What dreary wastes those are when we look back. And let them consider that the United States began with a book. It was reading the Bible that brought a few hundred people to these shores. From their reading came the cabins and farms, the towns, and great cities. It was poetry that started all that.

The task of the poet is to bring people back to reality—to dispel the illusions provided by daily living, as though to labor, eat, and sleep were all; to dispel the illusions provided by the state—at their worst, such illusions as are forced upon the people by a Stalin, a Hitler, a Mao Tse-tung. Poetry returns us to seeing and hearing. What we see and hear may not be pretty but it's true. This is, in the words of a poet, "where all the ladders start, / In the foul rag-and-bone shop of the heart." We are besieged by illusions; those of us who teach are particularly besieged, for we deal in ideas. The carpenter who comes to fix the roof, the man who fills your gas tank, is not likely to be confused by ideas. But we, the so-called educators, receive ideas from every direction and are in danger of not knowing what to believe. This is where poetry comes in: it brings us back to our perceptions and our sense of the real.

Beyond this, poetry, to quote Conrad again, reaches "the secret spring of responsive emotions." In so doing it wakens in our hearts a feeling of solidarity, "of the solidarity in mysterious origin, in toil, in joy, in hope, in uncertain fate, which binds men to each other and all mankind to the visible world." That feeling when we write, or read, or listen to a poem is the better world we envision. In poetry it is happening here and now.

Index

UNDER DISCUSSION
Donald Hall, General Editor

Volumes in the Under Discussion series collect reviews and essays about individual poets. The series is concerned with contemporary American and English poets about whom the consensus has not yet been formed and the final vote has not been taken. Titles in the series include:

Elizabeth Bishop and Her Art
  edited by Lloyd Schwartz and Sybil P. Estess
Richard Wilbur's Creation
  edited and with an Introduction by Wendy Salinger
Reading Adrienne Rich
  edited by Jane Roberta Cooper
On the Poetry of Allen Ginsberg
  edited by Lewis Hyde
Robert Creeley's Life and Work
  edited by John Wilson
On the Poetry of Galway Kinnell
  edited by Howard Nelson
On Louis Simpson
  edited by Hank Lazer
Anne Sexton
  edited by Steven E. Colburn
James Wright
  edited by Peter Stitt and Frank Graziano
Frank O'Hara
  edited by Jim Elledge
On the Poetry of Philip Levine
  edited by Christopher Buckley
The Poetry of W. D. Snodgrass
  edited by Stephen Haven
Denise Levertov
  edited by Albert Gelpi
On William Stafford
  edited by Tom Andrews

Forthcoming volumes will examine the work of Gwendolen Brooks, among others.

Please write for further information on available editions and current prices.

Ann Arbor   The University of Michigan Press